A COUNTRY TOWN

ITS PEOPLE & PLACES, FRIENDS & RELATIONS

A Buckingham sketchbook with stories by

ALAN PERCY WALKER

BARRACUDA BOOKS LIMITED
BUCKINGHAM, ENGLAND
MCMLXXXVIII

PUBLISHED BY SAGA
PART OF BARRACUDA BOOKS OF BUCKINGHAM, ENGLAND
AND PRINTED BY
M & A THOMSON LITHO LIMITED OF GLASGOW, SCOTLAND

BOUND BY HUNTER & FOULIS LIMITED
OF EDINBURGH, SCOTLAND

JACKET AND CASE PRINT BY
CHENEY & SONS LIMITED
OF BANBURY, ENGLAND

ISBN 0 86023 298 0

CONTENTS

CONFESSIONS & APOLOGIES

This book of pen & ink drawings and their attendant scribblings is of a Town I have known for only nine years (some of its villages a little longer), so I feel bound to apologise in advance to those readers who are more familiar with the Town, for they are certain to find some of their favourite places and stories missing from these pages. That the book is not more thorough is something I could blame onto lack of space, but it is fairer to say that a whole lifetime would be too short to do justice to an area so rich in material for both artist and writer.

This is *my* impression of the place and I am flattered that it has been published. I hope that no part of the book or its omissions offend anyone and that those not familiar with the Town and its villages find something here of general interest.

You will find that I have mixed anecdote with legend quite carelessly, and you should be warned that the boundaries between history and gossip have been blurred. I have been wilfully digressive throughout, and those reading it from beginning to end will find the whole lot no more profound than a chat in a pub. I hope you enjoy it.

THE HUBRIS OF THE LONG DISTANCE SCRIBBLER

Whilst a page of type, in Times Roman, may seem to have more authority than a whole book full of my handwriting which, I must say has been spruced up for the occasion, my 28,000 words are in my own script, not only because they assist in giving the impression of an informal sketchbook, but also because they allow me more control over the relationship between words and drawings. Generally, you will see the drawing about which you are reading, without having to turn a page.

So, quite recklessly, I have also taken two or three paces away from the advantages of a word-processor, and I have thrown away the author's prerogative of blaming the printer for all mistakes.

I await the first banana-skin.

† This is certainly not a textbook on drawing technique, but I have included a few notes about my approach to sketching with pen & ink. Those readers who are not interested can ignore the passages marked with these signs †

A VIEW FROM THE HARBOUR?

The subject of this sketchbook is a small English country town 80 miles from the estuaries of the River Severn, the River Itchen and the River Crouch, and 80 miles from the Wash. Buckingham could scarcely be further from the sea. It is one of the mid-points of England. Some say it is 'an average kind of place'; others have said 'very average', meaning mediocre. Like many a country town it has experienced periods of depression following the impoverishment or extinction of local aristocratic families, and this Town suffered especially, for it is the doorstep of a defunct dukedom which, at the height of its fortunes, was one of the grandest in the realm. Buckingham is typical in other ways. The Civil War left its scars; the Town and every one of its villages lost sons during two World Wars; until 1967 it was served by a railway; the average man can still have a laugh and a drink in a pub with a past, and now

BUCKINGHAM
R.SEVERN
R.CROUCH
R.ITCHEN

Buckingham is perhaps a little earlier than some in benefitting from the revival of the 1980s.

This is a drawing of a street renamed after the Battle of Trafalgar; the Fleet would find no anchorage near here but this is, however, a drawing of a waterfront. The river which ran alongside this road was redirected to make room for a large and ugly paint factory which, for many years, kept local men in work. In 1987 the business moved to a discreetly landscaped industrial estate and the building was demolished, making it possible, for a while, to see this panoramic view again. In 1725 a fire started along the left-hand side of this stretch and spread to other parts of the Town; consequently none of the buildings here, except a couple on the right, were built before that date. So, like the best of towns, Buckingham has had a Great Fire and can boast of a street named after Nelson.

Journey to a Country Town

For many people, their first journey to Buckingham was from London-Euston, leaving platform 6 and passing through the backyards of Regents Park and Hampstead, on to Bushey, Watford, King's Langley and Abbot's Langley, Hemel Hempstead and Berkhamsted; past the cricket ground set within the walls of a derelict castle and past the watercress beds beside the Grand Junction Canal; then through Tring to Cheddington, where few commuters alight at the wooden platform, propped high above the wheatfields which surround Mentmore Towers; then to Sears Crossing and a bridge near Linslade, scenes of the Great Train Robbery in 1963, changing at Bletchley Station which is about 50 miles to the north of London and a little to the west.

THE OLD STATION BLETCHLEY — NOW, MOST OF IT HAS BEEN MODERNISED.

The old railway town of Bletchley is now part of the new city of Milton Keynes, where factories are like giant tobacco tins, and where there are more road roundabouts per square mile than perhaps anywhere else on earth. At one time Bletchley was the intersection of the London to Birmingham railway and the east-west line from Cambridge to Oxford. Buckingham is 11 miles to the west of Bletchley and until 1967 trains steamed down the Oxford line to Verney Junction, which was another important intersection

A 'SUPER D' ON THE CAMBRIDGE TO OXFORD LINE

METROPOLITAN LINE

in its time, for this was the terminus of the Metropolitan Line out of Baker Street. From Verney Junction there was also a single-track branch line off the Cambridge-Oxford route; it ran northwards through pasture land to Padbury and Buckingham.

THE VERNEY ARMS

The topography of Buckinghamshire might have been very different for, during the founding of the railways in the 1820s, the main line from London to Birmingham was planned to pass through Aylesbury, thence (presumably) through Buckingham, but local landowners opposed its construction. The laying of the Buckingham line did not take place until the late 1840s, which forced the railway company to find an alternative route for their main line. Had the landowners been less obstructive, the heavy industry of Wolverton with its regimented rows of terraced houses, together with all the bustle of Bletchley, might have been situated in the meadows between Verney Junction and Buckingham.

VERNEY JUNCTION

The landowners were so peeved by the eventual arrival of the railway, they managed to delay the opening of a station

PADBURY STATION.

at Buckingham for a further 12 years. Even when it did open there were those who hampered the construction of an approach road, causing local travellers to start their journeys by tramping across ploughed fields.

BUCKINGHAM STATION

The station at Buckingham was demolished before my time, so this drawing is a reconstruction from old plans. The line through the Town is now a pleasant public walk, and Nature has been allowed to take over its verges and embankments. Buckingham Station was opened in 1850 and closed during the 'Beeching Cuts' in 1967. Now travellers to Buckingham must leave the train at Bletchley.

The A421 from Bletchley passes through grazing land and, in the early summer, there are also fields of brilliant yellow oil seed rape. Parts of this road are very straight, and Roman routes are known to have criss-crossed the high ground around Buckingham. But there is disagreement on whether they made use of Buckingham itself: some say 'Where's the evidence?' and there doesn't seem to be any. Others feel that the Romans would not have foregone the chance of exploiting the position —

THE OLD RAILWAY LINE ABOVE BATH LANE.

Buckingham is essentially a road junction and a river crossing. The Saxons certainly recognised its strategic value by building a castle there. Now, the site of the castle is occupied by the parish church, the spire of which comes into view as the traveller approaches the Lone Tree public house, so named because of the gallows tree which once stood at the cross-roads.

THE LONE TREE
NEAR THORNBOROUGH

From the Lone Tree the road drops, quite steeply for Buckinghamshire, and passes two Roman barrows which were opened up in 1839 and produced a valuable assortment of objects dating from the 2nd century AD. At the bottom of the hill is Thornborough Bridge. Until 1973, when a modern road-crossing was built a few yards away, this mediaeval packhorse bridge carried the increasing flow of traffic between the two towns.

THE ROMAN BARROWS

THORNBOROUGH BRIDGE

Its narrowness allowed only a single flow of vehicles and, because there were no traffic lights, motorists travelling in opposite directions were forced to come to an understanding. This was not a problem for most people, although there were some of a sporting nature who would drive down opposing hills hell-for-leather in a game of 'chicken' to see who would reach the centre first; he who lost reversed.

NEW TECHNOLOGY OLD ANSWER

In 1972/73 a new bridge was planned; the smooth curves of the new road crossed the river on the southern side of the old bridge. Just before its development an archaeological excavation revealed a road dating from around the 1st century AD, and that the engineers 19 centuries ago had selected the same crossing point.

About 80 yards to the south of the new bridge and on the west bank of the river, there is also the site of a small Roman temple. It is felt by some people that there is a lot more to be discovered in this area between Thornborough and Buckingham.

It is said by countrymen that hares of a particularly large size, with broad black-edged ears, roam the fields on the northern side of the road between here and Bourton. I have never seen one, but I am assured that I am not having my leg pulled.

Bourton is the only village on the road between Bletchley and Buckingham. It was never a large place and most of it, including the manor house, was razed during the Civil War. Now Buckingham has expanded and what is left of Bourton almost joins the Town.

Bourton Villa is set close

BOURTON VILLA, BUCKINGHAM

by the road and was built for a retired vicar some time between 1790 and 1805; he wanted a house in the style of villas he had seen in Italy from where he had recently returned. It is a design unique to north Bucks. Needlessly, the house faces east, with its back to both church and Town. Maybe it reflected the vicar's feelings.

In the garden of that house there was once a large elm tree; it was used for one of the last public hangings in the area. The victim was a 17-year-old boy, who had been found guilty of stealing sheep. The stump of the tree is still there and older people in the Town refer to this stretch of road as Gallows Hill.

In 1670 it was recorded that the return trip from Buckingham to London on the stage coach took 4 days.

Until 1805 the coaches crossed Sheriff's Bridge and entered the Town by the sign of the Woolpack Inn. For centuries sheep and wool were important, if not central, to the livelihood of Buckingham people. When Sheriff's Bridge fell into disrepair the road was redirected and a hostelry named the Jolly Yeoman was demolished to make way for the new London Road Bridge. Now the street which leads past the Woolpack Inn has only a footbridge, and the name Ford Street belies what is really there. One might

FORD STREET.

be able to cross the water in a Land Rover or on a horse, but now it is not intended as a crossing for ordinary vehicles. Close by the ford is the football ground of Buckingham's team, The Robins, which first 'leathered-off' in December 1883 against Banbury; the score was 0-0. In 1979 a bus carrying a visiting side was misdirected through the water. The river was running faster than usual, and the driver, who was not a local man, could not see that the road was broken, or how it shelved abruptly into deeper water. When the front wheels went over the edge the vehicle became buoyant and the flow of the river carried the bus downstream. The luggage compartment, containing the players' gear, became flooded, and for a while the visiting team were marooned. Also, the coach effectively dammed the river, causing the pitch to become flooded and the game to be called off. If the incident had been a ploy in one-upmanship by a local supporter, then it should be said that it did not work. When the game was eventually played, The Robins lost.

The ford is a favourite place for children, who gather there with jam-jars and minnow nets — others with bread for the ducks and swans. The grassy banks around the ford are home to about twenty rowdy mallards, one or two belligerent Aylesbury drakes and two charming old mute Muscovy drakes, who seem to know the opening times of Well Street's fish & chip shop and make their way there to appeal to customers.

ANOTHER JOURNEY

like the A421 through Bletchley, the A422 also leads to Buckingham from Watling Street.

The Watling Street of the Midlands has long been regarded as the frontier agreed between Alfred and the Danes in the Treaty of Wedmore. From Marble Arch to St Albans, Towcester to Telford, Shrewsbury to Betws-y-Coed and Bangor, through Anglesey to Holyhead, for decades this road has been known as the A5. But since the founding of the new city of Milton Keynes the planners have redesignated their short stretch, which runs between Fenny Stratford and Stony Stratford as the 'V4', which has bewildered more than a few travellers.

A COCK & BULL STORY

For a long time, Stony Stratford was an important stop for travellers along Watling Street. Two of its inns, the Bull and the Cock, were favourite meeting places for coachmen, many of whom enjoyed a drink or two, and a gamble on the cockfights which took place among the stables, the ostlers' sheds and outbuildings at the rear.

The stories they told of their exploits and of their variable luck around the fighting pits were said to have been embroidered with each telling. Sometimes their tales were so fanciful that the term "a cock-and-bull story" referred to any tale of dubious authenticity. Recently it was suggested to me in Stony that this story itself might be described as one of them.

WATLING STREET
STONY STRATFORD.

The A422 leaves Watling Street just north of Stony Stratford at a small place known as Old Stratford. The road to Buckingham passes to the north of the old hamlet of Passenham, then to the south of Deanshanger — a red and dusty village dominated by an oxide works and its smoke.

THORNTON HALL

This stretch of road is in Northamptonshire; then, no sooner back in Bucks, it passes the lodge gates of Thornton Park where, it is said, a manor house has existed for a thousand years. In the fourteenth century a chantry chapel was founded in the little Church of St Michael situated close to the house. The deeds here require the owner "to find a priest for ever, to the intent to say Mass daily in the church .. and to teach the children.".

✝ I used an ordinary 12p Bic ballpen for this drawing. They are quick to use, so they are excellent for foliage; but if you are not careful they blob. ✝

Some have claimed that the Hall was blighted, for there was a time when it was seldom inherited by a male heir. The last family arms to be emblazoned in the great hall are those of Cavendish – the family name of the Dukes of Devonshire. Now the Hall is The Convent of Jesus & Mary – a boarding and day school for young ladies. The estate is farmed independently – the meadows by the River Ouse are generally used for grazing sheep; the higher land is now down to cereals, and here and there thick rectangular blocks of woodland which bustle with wildlife.

Past the gates of Thornton Park, the road winds and drops almost to the level of the River Ouse; then, just over the brow of the next hill, there is a narrow turning to Leckhampstead Wharf and Thornborough. The field beyond, which is large and often filled with sheep, rises again and drops to Hydelane Farm. This field attracts lapwings; the local name is peewit. Once when I sat sketching by this field I watched three sheep dogs, one elderly, two quite young, making a professional job of driving the sheep down to Hydelane Farm — some 600 yds away. When they were almost out of sight the old dog stopped and seemed to be looking back towards me; then he left the two younger ones to carry on with the sheep while he made his way back to the top of the field, stopping every 30 yds or so to reconsider his tactics. Unintentionally I had been the cause of his fruitless return, because I had parked my white car within his view, and it was not until he was close to it that his failing eyesight allowed him to see that the car was not the errant young tup he had imagined.

When it arrives in Buckingham this road is known as the Stratford Road; it passes the site of the Town's old workhouse, now totally demolished, and runs alongside the sturdy iron pens of the old cattle market, now a car park and bus stop. Here the road is joined by another route from Watling Street — the Towcester Road.

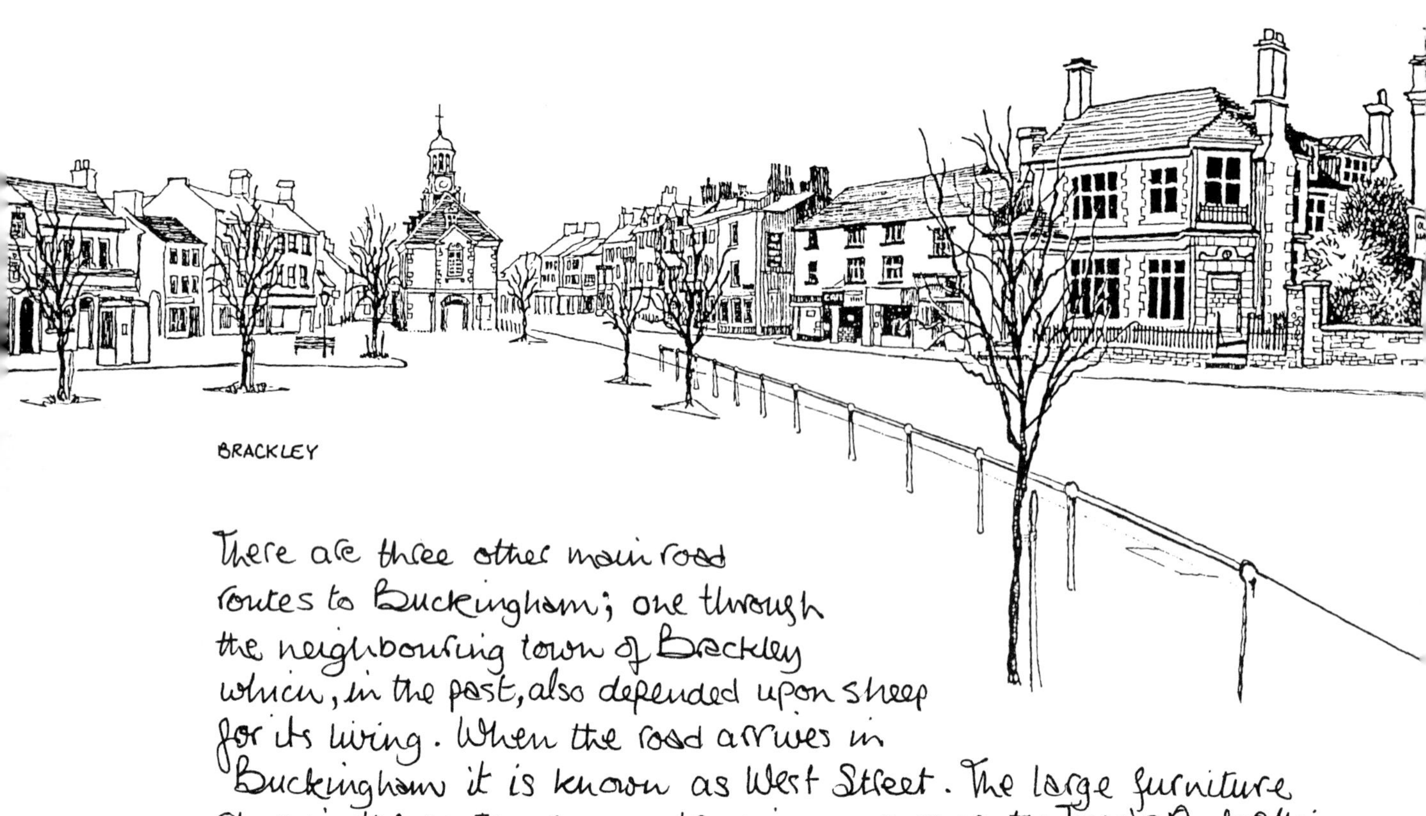

BRACKLEY

There are three other main road routes to Buckingham; one through the neighbouring town of Brackley which, in the past, also depended upon sheep for its living. When the road arrives in Buckingham it is known as West Street. The large furniture shop in the centre of my drawing was once the Town's Post Office and adjoining that there was once a grocer's shop. The proprietor is said to have been a man of considerable presence and persuasion for, I'm told, he would tour the villages on his horse, brow-beating cooks and housekeepers at the larger houses, or hob-nobbing with the gentry and shaming them into placing orders larger than their neighbours'.

Before that it was the Cobham Arms Inn, which featured significantly in the Town's role as servant to some very eminent and hospitable Dukes.

WEST STREET, BUCKINGHAM

THE ROAD FROM OXFORD

SHEEP STREET AND THE MARKET SQUARE BICESTER

From Oxford, the main road route to Buckingham is through St Giles and Summertown, turning right at Kidlington, passing at a tangent another old sheep town — Bicester — using the A421, at this point a Roman road. At Finmere it joins another route which has its origins in the Cotswolds — Stow-on-the-Wold and Chipping Norton. On its way to Buckingham the road passes through the centre of Tingewick — an attractive village now shaken continuously by a monstrous flow of heavy traffic.

TINGEWICK

The road then rises as it passes the Town's golf course and just over the brow Buckingham comes into view — hazy and half hidden in its valley, presided over by the parish church on Castle Hill. Until 1987 travellers down this road might have good reason to believe the church spire looked a little wonkey.

NELSON STREET AND St. RUMBOLDS LANE WITH THE CHURCH OF St. PETER & St. PAUL AFTER RESTORATION.

The final main road route is from the south, for centuries an unpopular way to Buckingham, for it crossed marshy ground and travellers frequently found the road difficult, sometimes impassable.

AIRPORT

Throughout the 1970s people from this area — the villages of Wing, Cublington, Stewkley, Hoggeston, Whitchurch and others — had to fight the threat of a third London Airport on their doorsteps. Many would have lost their homes completely. Feelings ran high and there was an effective campaign against the plans. Roads were lined with posters and signs, some quite large, such as this one on the approach to Winslow.

NO

The small town of Winslow is built on higher ground; only 6 miles from Buckingham. The names of the two are often spoken in the same breath. Traditionally, 'Buckingham & Winslow' have done together the things they were sometimes too small to undertake separately; jointly they founded associations— — The Buckingham & District Round Table, etc; together they are covered by the same local press.

Winslow Hall stands high and looks south across pasture land toward the Chiltern Hills. Once it was thought the Hall had

WINSLOW HALL

been designed by Sir Christopher Wren; the claim was based to some extent upon an entry in the ledgers of the banking family Lowndes, for whom the Hall was built. It is said that an outstanding loan to Wren was deleted from their books at about the date the house was built. Now authorities believe that Wren was not responsible for its design, but that maybe it was the work of a junior architect in Wren's employ – which would account for the accounting.

The principal rooms are gathered around a massive central core of chimneys, an idea often used in the construction of more modest country houses. Winslow Hall is currently the home of Britain's retired ambassador to Paris, Sir Edwin and his wife Lady Tompkins.

The road from Winslow touches the village of Padbury and enters Buckingham by the same route as the road from Bletchley, across the London Road Bridge, up Bridge Street to the old Town Hall.

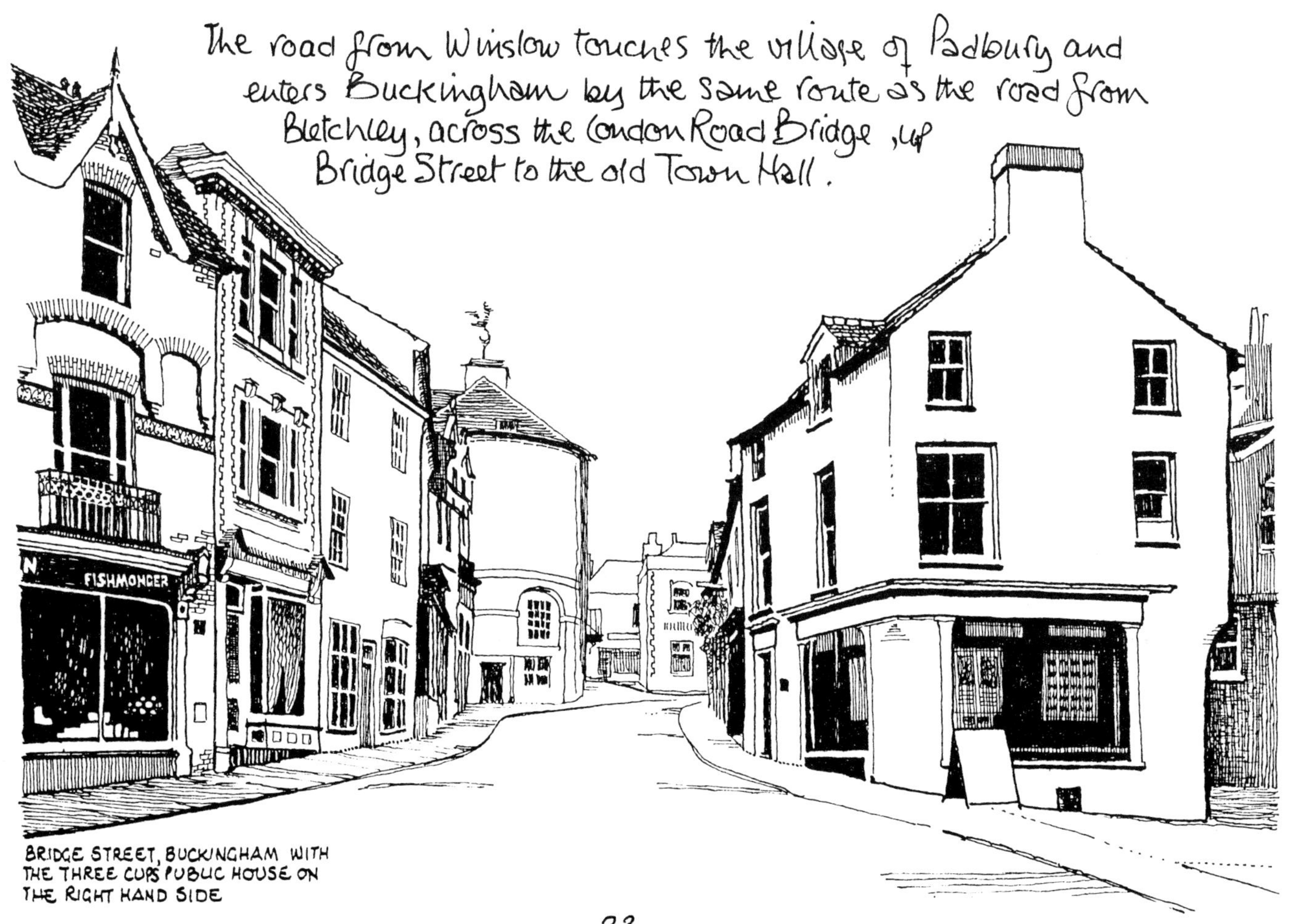

BRIDGE STREET, BUCKINGHAM WITH THE THREE CUPS PUBLIC HOUSE ON THE RIGHT HAND SIDE

TO BUCKINGHAM BY BOAT

There is a Buckingham Canal which is known to millions and it runs for about 150 miles, parallel to the Coromandel Coast, starting near Madras and running north beyond the point where the Gundlakamma flows into the Bay of Bengal. But the canal which once served Buckingham Town possessed little of the greatness of its Indian namesake. It was quite a mean little ditch – maybe one of the narrowest in Britain – and it ran for a mere 9½ miles.

There is evidence of it still throughout its length. But all that's left, with water enough to carry boats, is a short stretch at its junction with the Grand Union Canal; a cul-de-sac of moorings; a 200 yard stump is all that's left of the Buckingham Branch which was opened in 1801 with much hullabaloo and free beer for everyone at the Cobham Arms.

The hope had been that a canal might open up Buckingham for trade, at the same time providing the Town with a passenger service to Paddington. The junction of the Buckingham Branch with the Grand Union (also called the Grand Junction) is on the 'up-side' of Cosgrove Lock. The summer of 1976 was officially declared a period of drought and the narrow boat on which I was then living, was stuck there for weeks because, like many lockgates throughout England, they were chained and padlocked to conserve water. Early morning was a good time to see kingfishers and herons at their most active. My drawing of what remains of the Buckingham Branch shows it quite wide at this point, but further on and for all the way to Buckingham it was little wider than the average boat.

COSGROVE LOCK

The grounds of a large house reach to the north side, and on the south the old Tow path is now pegged out with moorings for pleasure craft. Cosgrove is not far from the Waterways Museum at Stoke Bruerne.

THE BUCKINGHAM BRANCH

The sound of hooves on towpath has long given way to the throb of large diesel engines, but still canals can offer an unforgettable spell of quietness and of calm at a pace which comes from the nineteenth century. Heartiness and cries of 'fore & aft', 'port & starboard' have always been out of place.

The Buckingham Branch followed the Stony Stratford road (A422) quite closely. It passed under Watling Street at Old Stratford. At Passenham the canal crossed to the north side of the road, then looped round Deanshanger to provide the factory with a wharf, and back to the south side to pass through Thornton Park where, by Act of Parliament in 1794, "in the reign of George III.. .. Thomas Sheppard Esq. of the Mansion House at Thornton ... was granted free liberty to use a pleasure boat upon the said canal".

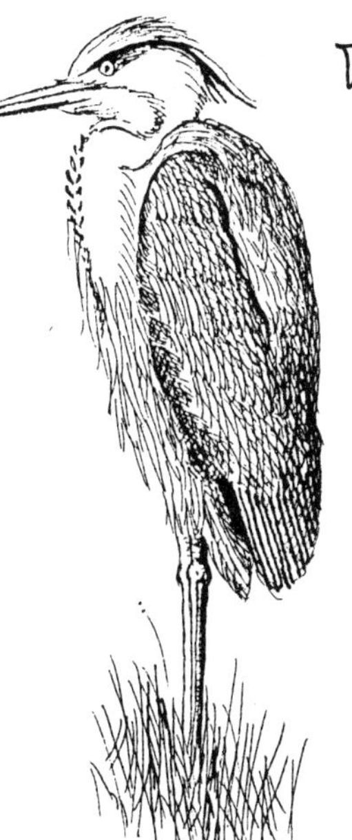

The course of the Buckingham Branch through the meadows near Thornton is still very clear to see and, because the canal was so narrow, farmworkers made do with a series of wooden swing bridges and plank drawbridges, some of which are still in situ. It is difficult to imagine, sometimes, that these pastures once saw narrow boats; that freight passed along the route between these grassy ridges. But it happened, and what is more it continued for over 100 years;

that is for a longer period than our roads have seen lorries.

There was a humpbacked stone bridge where the Thornborough Road crossed the canal, and beside this was built Leckhampstead Wharf. Alf Canvin, who lived at Thornborough and who worked on the canals when he was a boy, told me how one of his first jobs had been to unload a narrow boat by himself. The goods were heavy and in sacks. Steadily he removed them all day long, at the end of which he had only partly completed the task and was fiercely berated by his employer for the way in which he had tackled the job. Instead of removing the sacks little by little throughout the length of the boat, he started by clearing one end totally and was working his way to the other. The result was that one end was in the air, the other about to take on water, but more important the opposing forces of buoyancy and weight might easily have broken the boat in two. The canal certainly had its accidents – there was another man of the same generation who had been ostracised by his family most of his life because, one day, when he was young, he had worked under the

+ I've found that machinery and such things as trains and narrow boats are best expressed with large painted areas of black – no cross-hatching. Black suggests the weight and strength of iron. +

influence of a few beers, causing his fully laden boat to collide with another. Both boats were holed; his own was sunk — and so was he.

At the Buckingham end of the canal there were lockgates in the meadows, on the opposite side of the Ouse from Bourton. These fields have been used by a flock of swans — as an over night stop — for as long as memories allow. The 16th Jan, or there abouts, is one of their dates.

THE CANAL COTTAGES BY THE STRATFORD ROAD

The old lock house is still there and further on, a row of canal cottages is situated close by the Stratford Road. The canal went round what is now a football field, and finished at the basin terminus, which is now the yard between a petrol station and a tyre & exhaust centre. The house below was built beside the roadway to the basin.

During the winter of 1870 it was possible to skate all the way from the basin to Old Stratford.

+ I used a ·3 Ceramicron pen for these drawings. It does not need to be primed; otherwise it is just like using a technical pen (with no thick and thins). It is convenient for quick 'informal' sketches of this type, and it is permanent, unlike many felt-tip pens, so it is useful also for 'pen & wash' paintings. Even with informal sketches I still plan basic perspectives & proportions — in blue pencil if the drawing is to be reproduced +

STRATFORD ROAD AT THE ENTRANCE TO THE BASIN TERMINUS OF THE BUCKINGHAM BRANCH OF THE GRAND UNION CANAL

The nearest pub to what was the basin is still called the Grand Junction.

Like the canal system as a whole, the commercial success of the Buckingham Branch was frustrated by the development of the railways. For Buckingham, the railway arrived just 49 years later. But even so the Buckingham Branch was never used with great enthusiasm, and there were problems with silting-up. Also, there seems to be evidence that Buckingham Town Council never took the enterprise seriously.

Like the railway companies which were to follow, the canal companies had rights of compulsory purchase; so with few exceptions the canal companies owned the land occupied by their canals, towpaths and their service areas. When the Buckingham Branch was being planned and land prices were being negotiated, Buckingham Town Council somehow managed to retain the land ownership of the basin and the final stretch of the canal. Now, it seems that either the

SCANDAL! BUCKINGHAM UP TO ITS EARS

Council's original motive had been a little devious, or subsequent members of it acted surreptitiously because, after a time, the Canal Company became aware that the Buckingham Branch was inclined to silt-up more often than most. Several times they drained it and had to employ teams of men with shovels to clean it out. It must have been a nauseating job, and for some time the Town's people must have suffered a dreadful stench. It appears that the Council had sneakily arranged for all the Town's sewage to be discharged into their part of the canal — in the hope that it would be swept or dragged beyond their responsibility. The Company asked the Council to make other arrangements for the waste but the Council were defiant. Legal action against the Town Council was taken locally but failed. The draining and the shovelling continued until the Canal Company was exasperated and took the matter to the Chancery Court, eventually obtaining judgement.

Until the opening of a ring road around the Town in 1984 all road routes to Buckingham converged upon Cannon Corner.

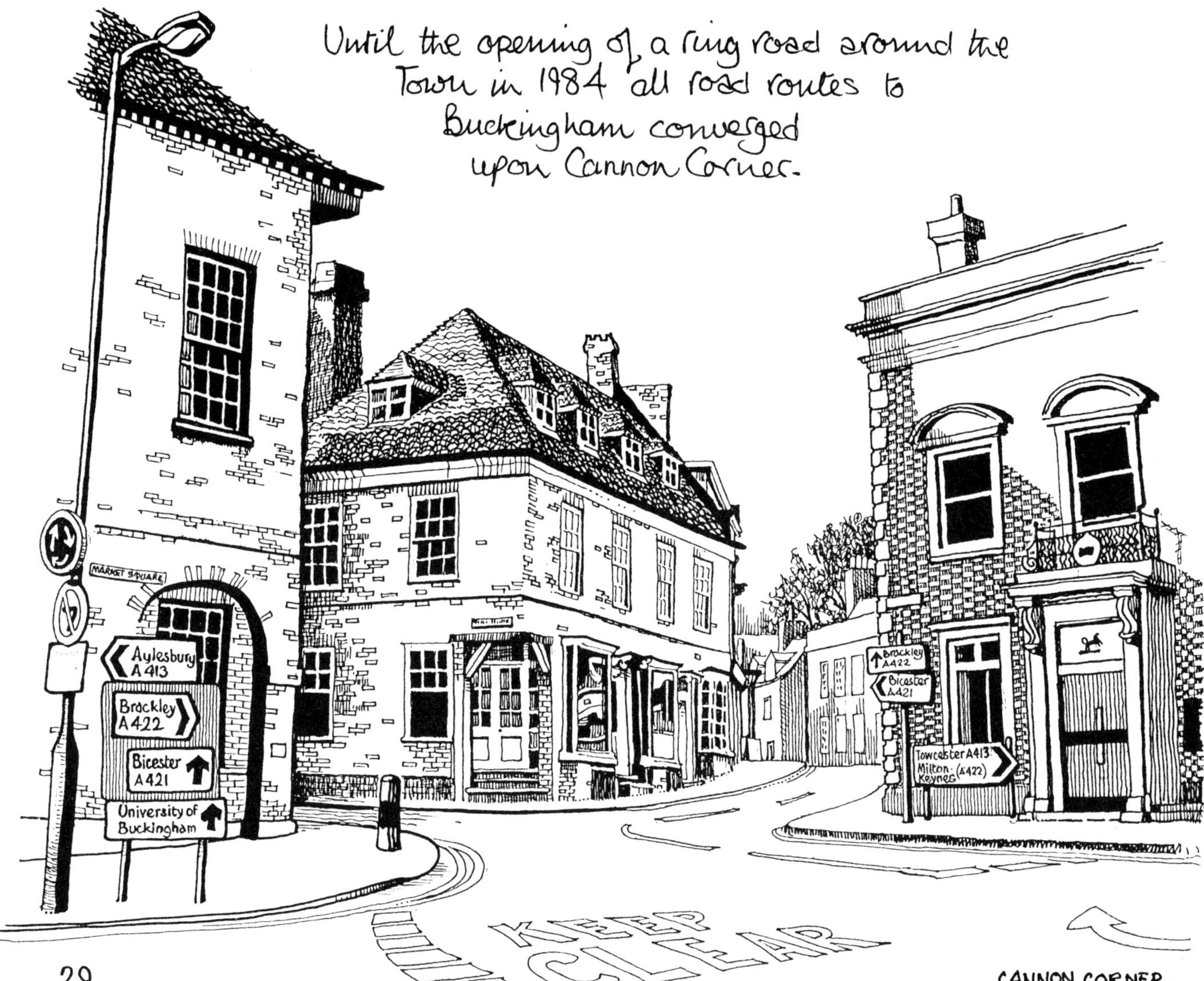

CANNON CORNER

A TIGHT CORNER

Grain lorries, brick lorries, trucks with beasts for slaughter, transporters carrying prefabricated silos or Sherman tanks, double decker 'buses, cars with caravans — everything converged upon Cannon Corner, causing some of the worst thromboses in the arterial road system of the South Midlands. The local newspaper, which was in the vanguard of the campaign for a ring road, had controversy and sensation delivered daily almost to its doorstep. With cameras and notebooks at the ready, reporters needed only to cross the Market Square to obtain further ammunition for their cause.

At one time Cannon Corner was even narrower, and during the nineteenth century it was found necessary to widen Castle Street by taking a four foot slice off the northern end of the Town Hall.

A TALENT FOR LOSING TOWNHALLS

However, the 'old' Town Hall we see today is not the first that Buckingham has had. There was an early lean-to structure erected in the ruins of the castle. Then in 1685 Buckingham was given its first 'proper' Town hall — probably at the expense of the Verney family. It is said to have faced the site of the present 'old' Town Hall.

Buckingham's seventeenth century town hall was conventional in design, consisting of a large room on arches and pillars. On top was a small clocktower. One might expect the Town to have been proud of its new possession and to have looked after it but, within 90 years, the cupola was in danger of falling in, and in 1783 the Town Hall had to be demolished. The present 'old' Town Hall was another gift to the Town, this time by the Temple family. Its secondhand roof timbers, which probably came from a building demolished on their estate, might have determined the awkward size of the building. The subsequent cutting back of its northern side resulted in the overhang we see today. The rounded end on the southern side is an addition and serves to increase the eccentricity of its overall appearance. Some of its internal features also come from an earlier building.

This Town Hall was certainly appreciated by people from miles around. For many years there were dances and concerts in the large ballroom on the first floor, where earlier this century a Wurlitzer organ was installed. Then in the 1970s history seemed to repeat itself. The Town Hall was declared to be against fire regulations and structurally unsafe. The District Council refused to restore it; instead they tried to sell it and agreed a price with a limited company which started to pay for it by instalments. Why the Council omitted to take a legal charge on the property until it was fully paid for, is not public knowledge. When the company defaulted, the Council sued too late and found that the Town Hall had been sold-on for a nominal sum, and the company had insufficient funds. Buckingham lost its Town Hall and the proceeds from its sale. This time the ratepayer was amongst those who came to the rescue – paying over £300,000 for a new Community Centre built in the flood meadows.

THE COMMUNITY CENTRE.

Buckingham has also been unlucky with its churches. The original Parish Church stood in what is now known as the 'old churchyard' — situated between Hunter Street and the Manor House. In 1699 its spire collapsed. Funds were raised for its restoration but seventy-seven years later it collapsed again, this time bringing down the tower. Then it was decided to build a new church on Castle Hill, largely

StMATTHEW Chapt VII 26 & 27

with materials from the old building and with some assistance from the Temple family. By 1781 an imposing new church had been completed but, within 80 years, this church too was in jeopardy of falling down. Severe cracks were appearing and on examination it was discovered that the foundations were unsound and had been inadequate from the start. It was necessary to erect a line of buttresses along the sides of the Church; these and the new windows between them are in the Gothic style (previously it had been a Classical building). Thus the Church was made wider; now the nave is flanked by additional aisles and seating. The chancel, another gift from the Temples, was added in 1865. There are several other indications that the eighteenth century Church was put together hurriedly and 'on the cheap'; today it is noticeable that much of the masonry which makes up

THE PARISH CHURCH OF St PETER & St PAUL

the tower was not properly faced to take the weather — a mistake unlikely to have been made by a master mason of repute. In 1987 more restoration work was undertaken. For some time it had seemed to many people that the spire was warped; it was bent at the top with an inclination toward the south as though under the influence of photosynthesis. When the top of the spire was removed it was found that the long iron rod which was set into the crowning masonry, and which descended through the centre of the spire to be securely bolted further down, had never actually received its thread. It had dangled, was unsecured, the top masonry unattached since 1781.

The third building, so easily remembered by those who have passed through the Town, is the Old Gaol. In the year 888, when King Alfred divided his Kingdom into shires he chose Buckingham as the County Town of a slender shire which stretched a long way south, beyond the Chalfonts and Burnham Beeches, to a point only 24 miles from the City of London. Centuries later Buckingham lost its countytownship to Aylesbury. The Old Gaol was built as part of an attempt to recover the Town's lost status.

THE OLD GAOL
1988.

THE BUCKINGHAM PALACE CONNECTION

For a town of its size the name of Buckingham is far more widely known around the world than one might expect. Who in Honolulu or in Hyderabad has heard of the county town – Aylesbury? But the name of the little market town of Buckingham is a very different matter. There is a tale that a man was brought before Buckingham magistrates charged with being drunk and disorderly. In Court it was explained that he had travelled all the way from Pakistan to Buckingham to see the home of the Queen of England. He enquired at various hostelries in the Town, the whereabouts of the Palace: eventually, bitterly disappointed, he drowned his sorrows. (The Magistrates, who were probably not really taken in by the tale, rewarded such an inspired defence by letting him off.)

But why _is_ the Royal Family's principal London residence named after a small country town in the South Midlands?

Answer: in 1703, when Buckingham was still a county-town (but only just), John Sheffield, who was a sailor and statesman, received the title Duke of Buckinghamshire & Normanby. At the time he was having a London home built in St James' Park — proud of his new title he named it Buckingham House. Fifty-eight years later, King George III, whose family was outgrowing St. James' Palace, bought Buck House from the Sheffields for £21,000. In the event it wasn't used a great deal by the Royal Family then, but in 1825 a new palace was begun on the site and Queen Victoria took possession twelve years later – naming it Buckingham Palace. The Duke left us a poem and some advice on our reading:

Read Homer once, and you can read no more,
For all books else appear so mean, so poor,
Verse will seem prose; but still persist to read,
And Homer will be all the books you need.

NOBLE RELATIONS

Several noble families have been associated with the Town, either by name, or with Buckingham itself. In addition to John Sheffield there have been three Ducal families – the Staffords in the fifteenth and sixteenth centuries; the Villiers in the seventeenth century; (Sheffield in the eighteenth century) and the Temples in the nineteenth.

The Staffords lived and died in turbulent times. The first Duke of Buckingham was killed not far from the Town, at Northampton fighting for King Henry VI. The second was beheaded for high treason in 1483 in the yard of the Blue Boar Inn at Salisbury; the scene is enacted in Shakespeare's Richard III. The third Duke met the same fate at Tower Hill in 1521. His lands, including the Manor of Bourton (now an environ of the Town) and the Manor of Buckingham itself, were confiscated and the title became extinct.

THE MANOR, BUCKINGHAM. Queen Elizabeth I is said to have stayed there.

Not much of sixteenth century Bourton has survived. The Manor House was razed during the Civil War – by Parliamentary supporters. There remains a pretty little farm bridge which may date from that time and a dwelling now called Rose Cottage which is said to be haunted by a friar. I lived there for a while but did not come across him.

'ROSE COTTAGE' BOURTON.

Then there were the Villiers: George Villiers was born in Leicestershire in 1592. He was to become a special favourite of James I. Young Villiers was dashing, handsome and accomplished; in a very short space of time he rose from being Sir George, to Viscount Villiers, to Baron of Bletchley (he had estates in Bletchley and at Whaddon). He had an extraordinary run of good fortune: he became Master of the King's Horse, and was appointed Lord High Admiral of England. In 1616 he was made Earl of Buckingham and the next year, Marquess. By 1623, a mere 31 years old, George Villiers became the Duke of Buckingham. He had been entrusted with the negotiations for the Royal marriage to the Infanta of Spain; later his own son spent much of his early boyhood with the young Prince Charles (King Charles II). There is a Van Dyke portrait in the Royal Collection showing the two boys together.

The Duke developed a fortune and he acquired from the Archbishop of York a substantial Thames-side residence, York House, close to Westminster; he founded Buckingham Hall at Cambridge (later renamed Magdalen College) and in 1626 he bought the whole of Rubens' private and very considerable collection of art. A sister of the Duke married into the Washington family, part of which later emigrated to America and produced the first President of the United States. Their family home was Sulgrave Manor, Northamptonshire - just over the county border from Buckingham. Needless to say perhaps, Sulgrave Manor now flies the Stars & Stripes and is open to the public. The Manor has furnishings from suitable periods of history, although probably few pieces were ever in the ownership of the English

SULGRAVE MANOR.

Washingtons. The kitchen of the house, so much admired by visitors, was brought lock, stock and barrel from another property in more recent times.

THE WASHINGTON ARMS.

The original arms of the Washingtons are carved into the stonework above the doorway on the south front; they consist of mullets & bars — stars and stripes. Appropriately for the USA's early years, 'mullets' are not stars of the celestial type but the rowels of a horseman's spurs.

VILLIERS STREET, BESIDE CHARING CROSS STATION.

Within a few years of being graced, Buckingham was losing his popularity — his extraordinary run of good luck also deserted him. He was assassinated in 1628.

His London home, York House, was demolished in 1675 but several of the streets and buildings which now occupy the site, adjacent to Charing Cross Station, are named after him. There are George Court, Buckingham House, Buckingham Street and Villiers House. If you walk from the Strand, down Villiers Street, past a pub called the Duke of Buckingham, you come to the Victoria Embankment Gardens which were established on land reclaimed from the River Thames in 1862. A few yards inside the gardens, now standing high and dry some considerable way from the water, is an old gateway. A notice there says it was built in 1626 for George Villiers, First Duke of Buckingham, to serve as a watergate to York House. His arms can be seen on the waterfront and his family motto on the landside, together with some anchor motifs to remind us he was once Lord High Admiral of England.

THE DUKE OF BUCKINGHAM'S WATERGATE TO THE THAMES.

RAKES & TROLLOPS

His son, also named George, succeeded to the title. It is said that he was a man of lively wit who, during his exile from Parliamentary Britain, cultivated the tastes and the haughtiness of French aristocracy. Throughout his life he held a passion for political intrigue and he was described by his contemporaries as restless, despotic, dissolute, profligate, malevolent.... This second Duke is said to have enjoyed his visits to Buckingham. The ruins of Buckingham's Saxon castle had been levelled and made into a bowling green (the site is now occupied by the Parish Church). Bowling was one of the favourite daytime recreations of the Duke and the party of sybaritic friends which usually accompanied him: their afternoon's bowling would be followed by a 100 yards stroll down Castle Hill to Trolly Hall. There they received sustenance and gambled into the night. The name Trolly is said to have been developed from 'trollops' — a local estimate of the character of the ladies who attended.

CASTLE STREET, BUCKINGHAM.
Trolly Hall is the house with the round window.

THE SOUTH FRONT OF CLIVEDEN.

In 1668 the Duke eloped with the Countess of Shrewsbury. Her husband, angered rather than heartbroken, pursued them and in a duel with Buckingham the Earl of Shrewsbury was mortally wounded.

It is said that Lady Shrewsbury, who had a slim boyish figure and, it seems, a vain inquisitive nature, arranged to witness the duel by dressing as a page and holding Buckingham's horse.

The Duke's attitude to the rest of mankind might be summed up in his own words — 'The world is made up for the most part of fools and knaves'.

His principal residence was in South Buckinghamshire, at Cliveden. The present house is of a later date, but the terraces, alcoves, and many of the walks would have been those used by the Duke when he courted Lady Shrewsbury.

The use of white gouache on a pen & ink drawing tends to give a ragged appearance to all the surrounding line work; often the result looks botched but it is a quick trick, for the lazy. I believe that all 'white' is best planned from the start, that each touch of black is made not for itself so much as for the whiteness it leaves around it. For this drawing I used a piece of printers' clay coated cartridge which enabled me to scratch away

some over-heavy pen work on the pavilion – using the paper like scraper-board. As with gouache it is useful to rectify mistakes, but I would not use it as part of the technique of sketching. In this drawing of the terrace at Cliveden I played a game with perspective. Panoramas produce interesting problems in the foreground. Sitting on the corner baluster I drew the terrace, the house, the patio, the tower and the Italian pavilion — swinging through an angle of about 110°. So the two balustrades, which in this drawing appear almost parallel, in reality are at right angles. Converging shadows are the result. But who noticed?

At the end of his life George Villiers was friendless, disgraced and penniless. He died in Yorkshire in 1687. After the sale of all his property there was not enough money to pay off his debts. He had no male heir and so the title once again became extinct.

INTRIGUE, PASSION AND INFIDELITY

In this century Cliveden became the home of Viscount Astor. His American wife, Lady Nancy Astor, became Britain's first woman member of Parliament and it was during that time the house lent its name to what the press called the Cliveden Set. Most of the famous names in literature & politics of the time were amongst the guests at Cliveden; although Winston Churchill was an occasional visitor, the politicians who gathered there in the 1930s were generally those associated with the policy of appeasement towards Germany.

The 1960s saw Cliveden in the headlines again. During a weekend party at the house, the Government Minister responsible for the Army was introduced to a young woman lounging by the swimming pool. She was slim, dark haired, and wore little save a smile of amusement. Her name was Christine Keeler and what she did not reveal to the Minister was that she was already having an affair with the Naval Attaché at the Soviet Embassy. The ensuing scandal left a trail of shattered reputations and ruined careers. It even threatened to bring down the Government. It was as though some spirit of devilment lingered at Cliveden. As if to remind us of its presence there is, cut into the turf at the west end of the terrace, the outline of a rapier and the date 1668. It commemorates Buckingham's duel at Putney when his mistress is said to have watched unmoved as her husband was being killed.

When the Astors left in 1966 Cliveden continued to have connections with the USA; until 1984 the house was leased to Stanford University of California. Now it is the property of the National Trust and the house is run as an hotel – attracting guests from the United States.

AT THE START OF THE DRIVE TO THE NORTH FRONT OF CLIVEDEN IS THE FOUNTAIN OF LOVE (1897) BY THE AMERICAN SCULPTOR THOMAS WALDO-STORY.

Lord Stockton (Harold MacMillan) was Prime Minister of the unfortunate Government at the time of the Profumo scandal; when told that Cliveden was to become an hôtel he said he thought that it had never been anything other.

THE DELIGHTFUL TEMPLES

The Temples were the fourth and the most recent of Buckingham's ducal families. They were closely associated with the Town and now, when local people talk of The Duke — they are usually referring to one of the Temples.

On high ground two miles or so to the north of Buckingham, and not far from the Northamptonshire border, is the parish of Stowe. There had been Temples at Stowe since the reign of Queen Elizabeth I. In the centuries which followed, the fortunes of the Temples rose: the family advanced from farming squires to Knights to Baronets, Viscounts, Earls, Marquesses and in 1813 Richard

Temple was made First Duke of Buckingham.

His great uncle, the Earl Temple who died in 1779, devoted 30 years of his life to making Stowe one of the Country's greatest homes. The Marquess of Buckingham who succeeded him brought great works of art to the house, and by the accession of Richard, the First Duke, Stowe was a truly splendid place, but before his death in 1839 the finances of the Temples were already a little shaky. Nevertheless, his 21-year-old son, also named Richard, the Second Duke, took Stowe to the zenith of its magnificence; but he over-spent.

There is a story in the Town that, when the Duke invited Queen Victoria and Prince Albert to visit Stowe in 1845, the court bailiffs had already established themselves at the house, making lists of the paintings and the silver. To avoid spoiling the Royal visit they agreed to wear the Duke's livery and to act as members of his household until the young Queen and her Consort had departed. The sale which followed realised £75,562 but the Duke was in debt to the tune of £1½ million. He left the country and died in 1861.

His son (all three Dukes were named Richard) took his responsibilities seriously and tried to do much to benefit the Town, at the same time working hard to restore his family fortunes. He died in 1889 without a male heir and so the Dukedom lapsed for the last time. His daughter, the Baroness Kinloss, whom some of the Town's older people can remember, let Stowe to the Comte de Paris — pretender to the French Throne — and for five years there was so much coming and going by his fellow countrymen that signs and notices at Buckingham Railway Station were duplicated in French. When the Comte died, Lady Kinloss returned to live at Stowe for a while. There is a touching photograph of her sitting alone under the vast portico on the south front, looking across her decaying estate toward the Corinthian Arch.

The heir to Lady Kinloss was killed in action during the First World War, and Stowe, the house and the estate, was placed on the market in 1921: in May 1923 it opened as an independent school for boys.

Stowe: south front.

From the Town, Stowe is approached up a long avenue of giant elms, the entire length of which might have fallen into the hands of property speculators in the 1920s, had it not been for the prompt action taken by Clough Williams Ellis – Stowe School's first architect, and creator of Portmeirion the fanciful village in north Wales. The avenue was sold separately some time after the main estate, and he bought it out of his own pocket, later passing it on when the school was better able to afford it. Dutch Elm Disease struck in 1970 and the trees were felled. The avenue has been replanted but it will be many years before it regains its old splendour.

On its way to Stowe the avenue passes the village of Chackmore. Today the road at that point bears left and skirts west around the estate. The unmetalled road used by the Dukes still leads to the Corinthian Arch but nowadays no further. At one time the road continued through the arch, turned left inside the grounds and passed across open meadows now used for grazing sheep.

At the height of its importance Stowe entertained the crowned heads and the aristocracy of Europe. This earlier approach to the great

THE CORINTHIAN ARCH, STOWE.

house was designed especially to impress them, and it was achieved with a fine sense of theatre. Guests arriving in their carriages would not see the house until they had passed through the Corinthian Arch on top of the hill. Turning westwards and gathering speed across open ground, visitors could peer through the side windows of their carriages and see, across the lake and still some way off, the magnificent south front of Stowe (even then not wholly visible, for trees were planted to obscure its full extent). Guests would have only a few moments to absorb the sight before they were conveyed through woodland to lower ground, and the vision disappeared.

THE OXFORD GATE, STOWE.

They would not see the house again until, with almost equal drama, they were brought to the north front. Today, the public road takes the visitor around, outside the estate to the Oxford Lodge, designed by William Kent.

THE BRIDGE OVER THE OXFORD WATER

Inside, the drive passes over a small bridge which spans the Oxford Water, an artificial feature, then up the hill between the two Boycott Pavilions. Designed by James Gibbs, these pavilions once formed the inner gateway to the park. At the top of the hill there is a straight avenue on level ground which follows the course of a Roman Road until it turns sharply right through a spinney to the north front – so high and hedged in by its colonnades that it is usually in shadow. Now, denuded of its statuary and ornaments, the north side can look forbidding, although it can look a more welcoming sight at night when lights are showing from the windows.

THE SOUTH-EASTERN OF TWO BOYCOTT PAVILIONS.

There is a tangled connection between the family name, Temple, their great passion for ornamental buildings, and their motto: (TEMPLA QUAM DILECTA) 'How delightful are thy temples'.

The present house was started on the instructions of Lord Cobham and it was designed by Sir John Vanbrugh. But for many years, even with its splendid collections of art, Stowe's fame rested principally with its gardens and their ornamental buildings.

THE CHINESE MUNTJAC

It was at Stowe that Charles Bridgeman, followed by William Kent, brought about a revolution in the art of landscape gardening. They broke away from the symmetry of the formal garden, its sharp geometrical shapes, and allowed beauty to be formed by the flow of nature itself. Then, the ha-ha allowed the surrounding country-side, as far as the eye could see, to become part of a grand design. This was possible at Stowe because the Temples owned the country-side as far as the eye could see.

THE DORIC ARCH.

Small muntjac deer, (a breed originally from S.E. Asia) were amongst a variety of breeds, some brought to Stowe to become part of the view beyond the ha-ha. The muntjac has an extra-ordinary way of running with its head held lower than the rest of its body: also they seem to be quite independent and do not live in herds as other deer. The descendants of the Stowe muntjac now roam wild for miles around.

STOWE CASTLE

It might be said that 'Capability Brown' served his apprenticeship at Stowe – he started as an under-gardener at the age of 24, rising to head gardener, during which time he was responsible for carrying out many of Kent's avant-garde designs.

One of the contrived views through the park and beyond is 'framed' by the 'Doric Arch' – erected in honour of Princess Amelia, a daughter of George II.

Through this arch can be seen woods and water and the Palladian Bridge. At one time a farmhouse could be seen in the distance, and it was during Kent's time that this was made to resemble an ancient castle.

Battlemented on the Stowe side, lean-to farmhouse on the other, Stowe Castle near Akeley Wood is another of the Temples' garden ornaments.

STOWE CASTLE

THE PALLADIAN BRIDGE.

Nowadays the Palladian Bridge is a favourite backdrop for group photographs of the departing sixth formers of Stowe School. These are not the first to regard the Palladian Bridge as a suitable location for filming. In 1948 J. Arthur Rank used it in a film called 'Trottie True', and since then Stowe has been used by another movie company, for a different type of film.

THE GOTHIC PAVILION.

In 1975, in common with other independent schools, Stowe set about increasing its income by opening the house and grounds during school holidays. Also it allowed the public to join sports clubs and use some of the school's facilities at certain times during term. Various functions are held at Stowe, including holiday courses and summer balls. It is possible, for example, to rent the Gothic Pavilion for a week at Christmas and have the party of a life-time.

STOWE. THE NORTH FRONT WITH A PORTE-COCHÈRE BELOW THE PORTICO FOR CARRIAGES ARRIVING IN THE WET.

It was in the 1970s, during school holidays, that the north front of the house and the marble hall were made available to another film company. There was some embarrassment soon after. Apparently, there had been no scrutiny of the script for, when the film was released the actress Fiona Richmond was seen making a stately arrival at the north front; her suitor in the story, a lusty debauched aristocrat, chased her up the steps into the marble hall where, I am told, a scene occurred which was not intended for 'family viewing', and which would certainly have upset Lord Longford and those similarly concerned with the 'erotic arts'.

Some of the pavilions on the estate are quite crudely put together

THE TEMPLE OF FRIENDSHIP.

and, like stage scenery, were intended to be viewed mainly from afar. This Lake Pavilion conceals a small dwelling by the Bell Gate – a tradesman's entrance to the great park.

ONE OF THE LAKE PAVILIONS

The Hermitage by the lakeside was built with one of its towers missing to give the false impression of antiquity. Now, it is used by the school as a boat-house.

To carry out Bridgeman's ideas in the eighteenth century, there was much clearing to do. A lot of the land which was to become Stowe Park was occupied by the villages of Stowe and Lamport – some of which had been destroyed during the Black Death and some sacked during the Civil War. However, in the eighteenth century, much of both communities was still in existence. Lord Cobham ordered the forcible removal of the villagers to Dadford and the demolition of their homes. Records of the two communities were also destroyed. Today very little of Lamport or of old Stowe remains.

THE HERMITAGE

The fourteenth century parish church of Stowe, which is situated close by the House, was only just saved from destruction and has been hidden by trees since the days of Lord Cobham.

The Church contains a window of engraved glass by Laurence Whistler. It celebrates the follies of the park which replaced the homes of Stowe's parishioners, and which almost deprived them of a place of worship.

THE COBHAM MONUMENT.

A monument to Lord Cobham was built during his lifetime. A tall column surmounted by his statue was erected on high ground to the north-east of the House. However, gravity and the elements conspired to make it difficult for the Viscount to retain his elevated position above the Parish of Stowe. Even at the time of its erection the monument was considered top-heavy and later, there was so much concern that the whole thing might topple, it was thought necessary to add a buttressing structure at ground level. Then in 1957 Lord Cobham's statue was struck by lightning; it fell in pieces and was beyond repair. Now it has been replaced by an urn.

Laurence Whistler had been a pupil at Stowe School as was Michael Gibbon, and together with George Clarke in 1956 they prepared the "Guide to Stowe's Gardens".

By the 1930s Stowe School was becoming part of the established

THE ROTONDO

way of things in England. Old Stoics were becoming Presidents of the Oxford Union and were winning the Sword of Honour at RMA Sandhurst. The School was visited by Edith Sitwell, Walter de la Mare, John Masefield, and G.K. Chesterton.

By the 1940s sons of old Stoics were arriving; by the '50s there were old Stoics in Parliament and by the '60s and '70s they were reaching 'maturity' and receiving knighthoods. In the September term of 1974 the first girls arrived at Stowe, and in the last decade it has been one of the most expensive independent schools in England.

THE EQUESTRIAN STATUE OF GEORGE I IN ROMAN ARMOUR. NORTH FRONT

However, in 1941 Stowe House was almost flattened: a lone enemy aircraft returning home unloaded its remaining bombs on what must have seemed an important target. The bombs landed in a row, starting just 200 yards from the south portico. There was no great damage done to the building.

During the Second World War 270 old Stoics lost their lives in the armed services. Of the 1900 or so who served, 46 were awarded the DFC, 111 the MC, 28 the DSO and two the Victoria Cross — one of whom was Wing Commander Leonard Cheshire who, when the conflict was finished, devoted his life to founding and running homes for the wounded.

In peace-time most old Stoics seem to settle into the relative obscurity of business, the professions or of the armed services. Some, however, become very well known.

A young man by the name of David Niven was amongst one of the first intakes at the school. Early on he acquired the nickname 'Podger' because of his plumpness - a condition brought on by his passion for milk chocolate. Then during a holiday trip to Piccadilly he met a young woman who, as he put it, "introduced me to the hurly burly of the chaise longue". His passions changed from chocolate to the attractive red-head whom he would secretly invite to Stowe. She would journey by train to Buckingham and picnic with young Podger in Stowe Park. She caused him considerable alarm on one occasion when, seeing the headmaster approaching, she insisted upon being introduced and on having a chat.

THE TEMPLE OF BRITISH WORTHIES

Christopher Robin Milne (son of A.A.) also finished his schooling at Stowe. George Melly was at the school during the war and entertained his House during their hours in the air-raid shelters. He especially liked his time at Stowe Art School, and George has since become one of the Country's leading authorities on surrealist art.

THE TEMPLE OF ANCIENT VIRTUE

David Shepherd, the painter famous for his pictures of African wildlife and for his collection of railway engines, was also a Stoic.

Richard Branson, of Virgin Records, was a more recent pupil.

STOWE, THE SOUTH FRONT.

The south front of Stowe is about 220 yards long and comprises, mainly, three pavilions unified by two galleries (a dining-room to the left and a library to the right). The design by Robert Adam was modified by a member of Lord Temple's own family and completed, in its present form, in 1774. The centre block contains an earlier house and the wooded area on the right conceals the old parish church.

THE GRENVILLE COLUMN — A ROSTRAL COLUMN TRANSFIXED BY THE PROWS OF GALLEONS

+ William Morris, in his letter declining to stand for election to Oxford's Chair of Poetry said '... it seems to me that the practice of an art rather narrows the artist in regard to the theory of it ...' George Bernard Shaw's oft quoted corollary of this (Those who can, do; those who can't, teach) is frequently and unfairly flung against well meaning teachers, but I believe there must be some truth in the notion. For there are certainly those with a talent for reciting established understanding and for recycling the thoughts of others; yet those who devote their time wholly to the practice of a craft are often speechless when asked to theorise. Words of theory are useful so far as they go, but I think there is nothing so advancing as a private and diligent study of the work of masters. For 'pen & ink' I look at the work of Walter Crane, Hullah Brown, Geoffrey Fletcher, James Priddey, Ronald Searle, Ronald Thelwell, Ray Evans ... and at the work of etchers, engravers & lithographers from Dürer to Whistler. +

The great portico on the south front of Stowe looks across the Octagon Lake toward the Corinthian Arch, and the grass close to the house is now marked out for rugby football. Chatham House, situated about 300 yards away also faces south and looks across the school golf course towards the Temple of Venus. The house was designed by Sir Clough Williams-Ellis and completed in 1926; it has a noble facade but its rear is like that of a London tenement.

CHATHAM HOUSE

Some of the masters who have taught at Stowe and some who are teaching there now, have also been the subject of headlines.

CAMELOT

T.H. White who was head of English in the 1930s, achieved fame with his novels 'The Sword in the Stone', 'The Queen of Air and Darkness', etc collectively known as 'The Once and Future King' from which the Broadway musical and the film 'Camelot' were produced.

Before taking up his appointment at Stowe in 1932 he had written novels such as 'They Winter Abroad' which at the time were considered risqué. He had no wish to be associated with them publicly, and he was anxious that his employers should not be embarrassed by them. So T.H. White used the nom-de-plume 'James Aston' which was an unfortunate choice; whilst he had a claim to the name (Aston had been his mother's maiden name), Tim White was unaware that there would be a boy named James Aston attending the school. Fan mail from readers, addressed to 'James Aston' c/o his London publishers, was usually bundled into a large envelope and forwarded to T.H. White Esq, Stowe School, but on one occasion someone at the publisher's office made a slip and the boy James Aston must have had an evening of fascinating reading.

THE CONGREVE MONUMENT.

Tim White's cover was blown: he could no longer dissociate himself from his fruity tomes. He resigned from Stowe and moved into a worker's cottage on a farm not far away and there he started writing in earnest. He wrote 'The Goshawk', and 'England Have my Bones' – an autobiographical book on his great loves; hunting, fishing, shooting and flying.

T.H. WHITE'S COTTAGE, BLACK PIT FARM.

Tim White, his red setter, his horse, his Bentley tourer, were all well known in the countryside around Stowe. He enjoyed some of the local pubs. When he finished writing the first book which was to make up the series known as 'The Once & Future King', he had almost run out of money. The book was his salvation. By the time he had written the third, 'The Ill-made Knight', and the final one, 'The Candle in the Wind' he was on the way to success and fortune. There is a biography of T.H. White, by Sylvia Townsend Warner; but when I was retracing his steps around the estate, talking to people who knew him and settling to draw this picture of his cottage, I had a feeling that there is a whole chapter of his life at Stowe which is unwritten.

Current Stowe author is housemaster Anthony Meredith, whose book 'The Demon and the Lobster' is about two leading cricketers of the nineteenth century — Charles Kortright, demon fast bowler for Essex and gentleman of leisure, and Digby Jephson of Surrey, a lob-bowler of distinction, poet and writer.

Composer Paul Drayton joined the music staff of Stowe in 1972. His work has been performed and broadcast throughout the world, in such varied locations as the Three Choirs Festival, Vienna, Tokyo, and the Hollywood Bowl, USA. His opera 'The Mellstock Quire', adapted from Thomas Hardy, was written in 1980 on a bursary from the Arts Council of Great Britain.

PAUL DRAYTON

Portrait sculptor William St A.R. Dady was Director of Art at Stowe from 1966 until his retirement in 1987; his talent for obtaining likenesses is considered by some to be amongst the finest in the Country.

Stowe Park is a treasury of monuments, temples, pavilions, grottoes, bridges, cascades.... and the genius of eighteenth century design at Stowe is ceaselessly enhanced by the spontaneous beauty of its plant life. I have drawn only a fraction of what is there; Stowe is worthy of volumes of its own — indeed John Piper was encouraged by Stowe's famous headmaster J.F. Roxburgh to produce engravings with a view to publishing a sequel to his Brighton Aquatints. After years of inactivity I gather it is now to be published by the Hurtwood Press in association with the Tate.

WILLIAM DADY

The most curious, to me, of all Stowe's ornamental buildings, is now not on the estate at all. The Park once reached to the Cobham Arms, which accommodated the retinue and friends of the more illustrious guests staying at the great house. In the garden of a bungalow at the rear of the old Cobham Arms is an eighteenth century summerhouse in its own walled garden and therefore not seen by many. Once it had a small and private doorway to the back of the hotel premises, and to the Town. Inside it is panelled and shelved as though for books or bottles, and at its entrance are two rustic figures set on plinths. For whose private moments or discreet liaisons it was built, can only be imagined.

✝ Loose work with a fine nib and a light hand can give a whimsical, aethereal effect ✝

The Earls of Buckinghamshire have not had much to do with the Town: the present Countess opened a fête in Buckingham in 1985 but their family origins are in Norfolk. Baron Hobart of Blickling, Norfolk was made the 1st Earl of Buckinghamshire in 1746. Blickling Hall had once been owned by Sir John Fastolf (the basis of Shakespeare's Falstaff), and later by Sir Thomas Boleyn, father of Henry VIII's queen. The Hall was purchased by the Hobarts in 1616 and it was reconstructed soon after by Robert Lyminge, who had been responsible for the building of Hatfield House. The earlier Hobarts were diplomats and colonial governors, the 2nd Earl an ambassador to Russia and later Lord Lieutenant of Ireland. By 1850 the estate was no longer in the hands of Hobarts, but I gather that most of the Earls of Buckinghamshire are entombed at Blickling and they have the distinction of standing rather than lying at rest.

BLICKLING HALL, NORFOLK. ONE MEMBER OF THE HOBART FAMILY WAS A VICE-PRESIDENT OF THE UNITED STATES.

FROM DUNGAREES TO ERMINE

In the 1960s, after the death of the 8th Earl, the title almost became extinct, but then a distant relative was discovered.

It was a cold day in January 1963; Vere Frederick Cecil Hobart-Hampden, a gardener working for Southend Council was clearing snow from municipal footpaths when he was approached by a stranger and to his astonishment informed that he might be a peer of the Realm.

The Upper House demands thoroughness in such matters and it took him some time to verify the claim. He took his seat as a Labour peer in 1967 and five years later, at the age 71, he married a lady from Australia. The present Earl, a cousin, is a sales director for a finance house, and he lives in Haddenham, Bucks — near Thame.

The saying that 'everyone loves a lord' might be disputed but it is certainly in the English character to have affection for an impoverished peer. On the road from Buckingham to Winslow lies the Addington estate where, for generations the Buskys were Lords of the Manor. There had been Buskys at Addington since the reign of Charles II; they lived and worked amongst their people; were not aloof from them; were not inclined to grandiosity. From stories I have heard, their estate was a model of both altruism and good management. A drained and gravelled pathway to the Town was maintained especially for the people who lived on the estate. It was a happy community with its own school, social club and well maintained dwellings which clustered in an area close by the big house. They bred some good cricketers and shared a ground with nearby Verney Junction.

Then in 1917 much of the family fortune was lost due to its substantial investment in the Russian railways. Lord Addington was forced to make many economies.

THE 'KISSING GATE' ENTRANCE TO VERNEY JUNCTION'S OLD CRICKET GROUND, BY THE FOOT CROSSING OF THE CAMBRIDGE-OXFORD LINE.

In more recent years Lord Addington would travel into Buckingham by local bus and was affectionately known by other travellers as 'Iron Gates' because, on his journey home, he would tell the bus driver to stop at the iron gates at the end of his drive.

The Addingtons no longer live there; many of the estate buildings have become privately owned houses and the cricket ground has given way to agriculture.

The Verneys first purchased land in the Claydons in the year 1463; of the sixteen or so Verneys who have owned the estate since then, eight have been named Ralph. The first Ralph was Lord Mayor of London and was knighted by Edward IV.

One hundred and thirty years later (five knights) there was a black sheep in the family. His name was Sir Francis; he sold off much of the family estates and property, then went to fight for the Turks in the Levant; he became a pirate, was taken prisoner and had to spend time as a galley slave before finally being ransomed.

THE ROYAL STANDARD BEARER

His unfortunate half-brother Edmund inherited a diminished and impoverished estate, but he was popular with the people at Claydon and attempted to restore the family fortunes. When King Charles I came to the throne, Sir Edmund Verney was appointed Knight Marshall of the Palace. In the Civil War he was the Royal Standard Bearer, and was killed during the Battle of Edgehill. Over 4000 men were killed that day and the body of Sir Edmond was never identified, but his severed arm was found on the battlefield, still grasping the Royal Standard. It was said that Sir Edmund's arm haunted Claydon House for over one hundred years.

CLAYDON MANOR AS IT MAY HAVE APPEARED BEFORE 1757.

For the remainder of the Civil War and during the interregnum, family life for the Verneys was shattered. The Claydon estate was sequestrated. Ralph, Sir Edmund's loyal son had to take refuge in France, his brother 'Mun' was murdered, his wife and sisters lived in poverty, and finally, his wife died trying to recover family property.

CLAYDON HOUSE AS IT IS TODAY — NOW A NATIONAL TRUST PROPERTY, THE VERNEY FAMILY CONTINUE TO LIVE IN A VICTORIAN WING ON THE SOUTH SIDE OF THE HOUSE.

With the restoration of Charles II, the estate was restored to the Verneys and, on his return from France, Sir Ralph was made a Baronet.

In time, his son Sir John became prosperous and was made 1st Viscount Fermanagh. In 1747 his son Ralph was created 1st Earl Verney, and it was his son Ralph, the 2nd Earl, who built the house we see today, but when it was completed in 1771 it was a much, much grander place.

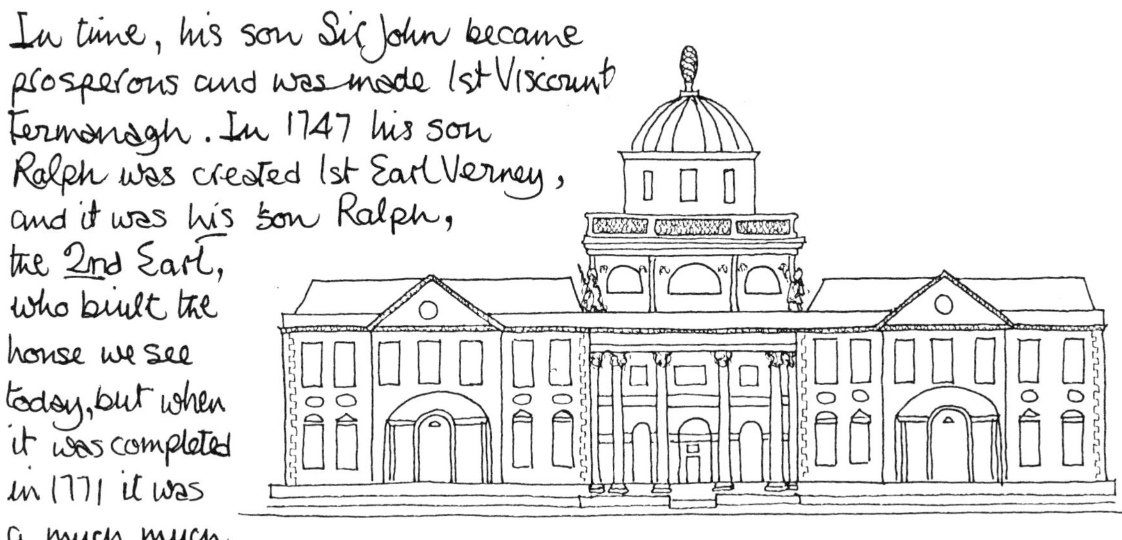

CLAYDON HOUSE AS IT APPEARED ON COMPLETION IN 1771, THE HUGE ROTUNDA AND THE WING TO THE LEFT WERE DEMOLISHED 21 YEARS LATER.

The house which was demolished to make way for it, and which survived for the Verneys throughout their troubles, and from long before, was a pre-Elizabethan manor house with stepped gables. Over the years it had been updated & embellished to conform to the fashions of the times. The 2nd Earl had a reputation for being generous, both to the needy and to the Arts; he was also flamboyant, even for an aristocrat of that period, and would travel the countryside in a coach & six, escorted by negro footmen announcing his progress with fanfares on silver horns. In building a great mansion at Claydon and furnishing it with works of art, he might well have been attempting to compete with his immensely wealthy neighbours – The Temples at Stowe.

The generosity and extravagance of Earl Verney led him to bankruptcy and he avoided imprisonment only by fleeing to France. Almost everything of value at Claydon was sold and the shutters of the great house were closed on empty rooms.

There is a tale that a son of one of the family's old servants one day peered through an open shutter and, to his surprise, saw the aged Earl wandering forlornly through the gloomy, echoing halls of his beloved home. It is said that the boy supplied his fugitive master with bedding and victuals, and kept him concealed there for some weeks.

A GRAFT ON THE FAMILY TREE

On the death of the 2nd Earl, in 1791, the title became extinct and Claydon was inherited by his niece, who ordered the immediate demolition of two-thirds of the mansion.

How succeeding owners of Claydon acquired the name 'Verney' is explained on a plaque displayed in the little church of All Saints, which is situated close by the house and which predates it by some centuries.

ON THE DEATH OF THE LAST EARL VERNEY, IN 1791, THE CLAYDON ESTATES, TOGETHER WITH HIS OTHER PROPERTY, DESCENDED TO HIS NIECE THE HONORABLE MARY VERNEY, CREATED BARONESS FERMANAGH ON HER ACCESSION TO THE PROPERTY, BY WHOSE WILL THEY WERE DEVISED TO HER MATERIAL HALF SISTER, CATHERINE, WIFE OF THE REV^D^ ROBERT WRIGHT DAUGHTER OF RICHARD CALVERT ESQ. OF NINEASHES IN HERTS, WITH DIRECTION THAT SHE SHOULD TAKE THE NAME & ARMS OF VERNEY. ON HER DEATH IN JAN. 1827 THE CLAYDON ESTATES DESCENDED BY VIRTUE OF HER WILL TO HER COUSIN AND RELATIVE, CAPT. SIR HARRY CALVERT, BARONET OF THE GRENADIER GUARDS ELDEST SON OF GENERAL SIR HARRY CALVERT, BARONET GCB & GCH IN WHOSE FAVOR THE WILL WAS MADE BUT WHOSE DEATH OCCURRED THE SEPT PREVIOUS. PURSUANT TO MRS VERNEY'S DIRECTIONS, CAPT SIR HARRY CALVERT OBTAINED HIS MAJESTY'S PERMISSION TO TAKE THE NAME OF VERNEY AND TO BEAR THE ARMS OF VERNEY, QUARTERED WITH HIS OWN.

Sir Harry Verney, who inherited Claydon in 1827, was MP for Buckingham for many years; he married Parthenope Nightingale, who edited the four volume Memoirs of the Verney Family which is now considered a classic record of the fortunes, adventures and adversity which befell a landowning family over four & a half restless centuries.

THE LADY OF THE LAMP

Lady Verney's sister was Florence Nightingale. From a distance, Miss Nightingale's Scütari looks like a child's sand castle. My little drawing of it on the hill by Üsküdor is from Istanbul – looking across the Bosperous towards Asia. My brief attempt some years ago to make a closer sketch of what is now known as the Sultan Selim Barracks, was cut short when someone from inside ordered a member of the guard to send me packing.

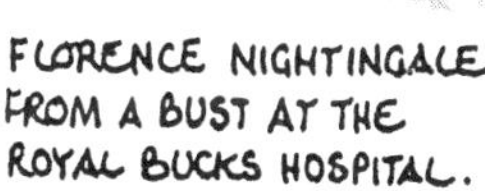

FLORENCE NIGHTINGALE FROM A BUST AT THE ROYAL BUCKS HOSPITAL.

Sir Harry's position as a long-serving and influential Member of Parliament was of assistance in Miss Nightingale's causes and ambitions. In her later years she spent much time at Claydon and in the museum on the first floor of the house there are showcases of her belongings, and photographs of her at Scütari. A bedroom there is now known as 'Miss Nightingale's Room' but, contrary to the impression given, she did not always stay at the house when she visited Claydon.

SCUTARI

Whilst no doubt the Verney family made her welcome, Miss Nightingale was not an 'easy-going' person and it is said that, when she stayed at Claydon for extended periods, she was given an isolated farmhouse on the estate.

Her lectures on hygiene, with a team of instructors, to village women around the County, were not always well received. However, the villagers of Steeple Claydon were grateful for Miss Nightingale's founding donation for the establishment of one of the Country's first community free libraries. In 1985 when the County Council planned to replace it with a mobile service the villagers fiercely defended it and the Council backed down.

The 'Claydons' consist of Steeple Claydon, East Claydon, Botolph Claydon, Middle Claydon and, of course, the very small hamlet of Verney Junction which, for over 100 years, linked not only North Bucks to Oxford and Cambridge, and the central

THE OXFORD TO CAMBRIDGE LINE AT VERNEY JUNCTION – BASED ON PHOTOGRAPHS TAKEN IN THE 1950S, WITH SOME OF THE GARDEN DETAIL IMAGINARY ON MY PART. BY ALL ACCOUNTS THE PLATFORM GARDENS AT VERNEY JUNCTION WERE VERY WELL KEPT AND FURNISHED WITH GNOMES & MODEL WINDMILLS AS I'VE TRIED TO SHOW. THE RAILWAYMEN AT BUCKINGHAM DID SIMILARLY AND THERE WAS SOMETHING OF A COMPETITION GOING ON.

rail system of Britain, but also connected Buckingham and the north of the County directly with the London Underground system. If the services had not been cut it is likely North Bucks would have developed into another London suburb, and the rise in property prices around the Town during the 1980s would have been much greater and occurred much sooner.

A Stroll Around The Town

A flock of pigeons holds court on the roof of Buckingham's old Town Hall and looks down on the Market Square which lies immediately below, flanked on one side by Lloyds Bank and on the other by the White Hart Hotel. Like the Cobham Arms the White Hart was once part of the ducal estate, and the Market Square was regarded as the centre of the Town. Now it is not recognisable as a square for it is marked out as a mini-roundabout in an effort to ease the flow of traffic at Cannon Corner — so named because a cannon was once set into the ground there; pointing skyward it acted as a bollard, but it was felled by a lorry in the 1970s.

At one time the White Hart had a coaching entrance and the London Stage approached the hotel from the rear. In 1871 the archway was enclosed and a front portico added. When the Town Hall became privately owned, the White Hart's portico was used for announcing the results of Parliamentary elections.

Earlier in the nineteenth century Benjamin Disraeli visited Buckingham and used the Town Hall at

election time. In the 1980s, when the old Town Hall was converted into a

UNTIL 1738 HUGHENDEN WAS A SIMPLE FARMHOUSE, THEN IT WAS MADE INTO A 'GENTLEMAN'S RESIDENCE' AND BENJAMIN DISRAELI CONTINUED THE TRANSFORMATION WHEN HE BOUGHT THE ESTATE IN 1848. HE GOTHICIZED THE HOUSE, GAVE IT A PARAPET TO OBSCURE THE ROOF, THEN ADORNED IT WITH PINNACLES. HE CONTINUED IMPROVING AND DEVELOPING HUGHENDEN THROUGHOUT THE YEARS LEADING TO WHEN HE BECAME PRIME MINISTER IN 1868. IT WAS WHILE HE LIVED AT HUGHENDEN THAT HE WROTE 'LOTHAIR' AND 'ENDYMION'. QUEEN VICTORIA VISITED THE HOUSE IN 1877 AND AGAIN WHEN DISRAELI DIED IN 1881. AT HIS FUNERAL THERE WAS A WREATH FROM THE QUEEN ENTIRELY OF PRIMROSES – SHE KNEW OF HIS GREAT AFFECTION FOR THE SIMPLE LITTLE SPRING FLOWER WHICH ADORNED THE SLOPES AROUND THE HOUSE. AFTER HIS DEATH HIS NEPHEW ADDED TWO WINGS TO THE HOUSE, REPLETE WITH PINNACLES, TODAY HUGHENDEN MANOR IS OPEN TO THE PUBLIC AND THE MORE RECENT WINGS ARE USED AS A DIVISIONAL OFFICE FOR THE NATIONAL TRUST. PRIMROSES STILL FLOWER AROUND THE HOUSE AND ON BENJAMIN DISRAELI'S GRAVE BESIDE HUGHENDEN CHURCH. AT THE NORTH FRONT OF THE HOUSE THERE IS AN ARCADED PORCH WHICH CONTAINS TWO WHITE MARBLE STATUES — ONE OF BENJAMIN DISRAELI, EARL OF BEACONSFIELD. THE SCULPTOR WAS C.B. BIRCH. THE ARCADE IS GLAZED AND WHEN THE SUN IS IN THE SOUTH THE STATUE IS VISIBLE THROUGH THE DARKNESS OF THE PORCH WHILE THE PLATE GLASS REFLECTS SUNLIT GROUNDS. THE RESULT IS DISRAELI'S APPARITION STROLLING THROUGH HIS BELOVED HUGHENDEN.

ruie bar, it was given the name Dizzy's. Disraeli lived at Hughenden Manor near High Wycombe, Bucks. In 1763 Buckingham actually provided the Country with a Prime Minister – namely George Grenville, who was the brother of Earl Temple. His 2 years in office were disastrous. It was the Grenville Administration which first proposed taxing the American Colonies. So it might be said that it was a Buckingham man who had a big hand in *causing* the American War of Independence and it was George Washington whose origins were also in the Buckingham area who brought the war to such a lasting and significant conclusion. In the early 1970s the constituency of Buckingham included Bletchley and the area now known as Milton Keynes. The Member was Robert Maxwell (Capt. Bob of the Daily Mirror etc), Labour. The seat was then taken by Bill Benyon, Conservative. The new city grew and for a time election results were announced from a public hall in Bletchley which had the greater concentration of voters. However, when the constituency boundaries were re-defined, Bill Benyon

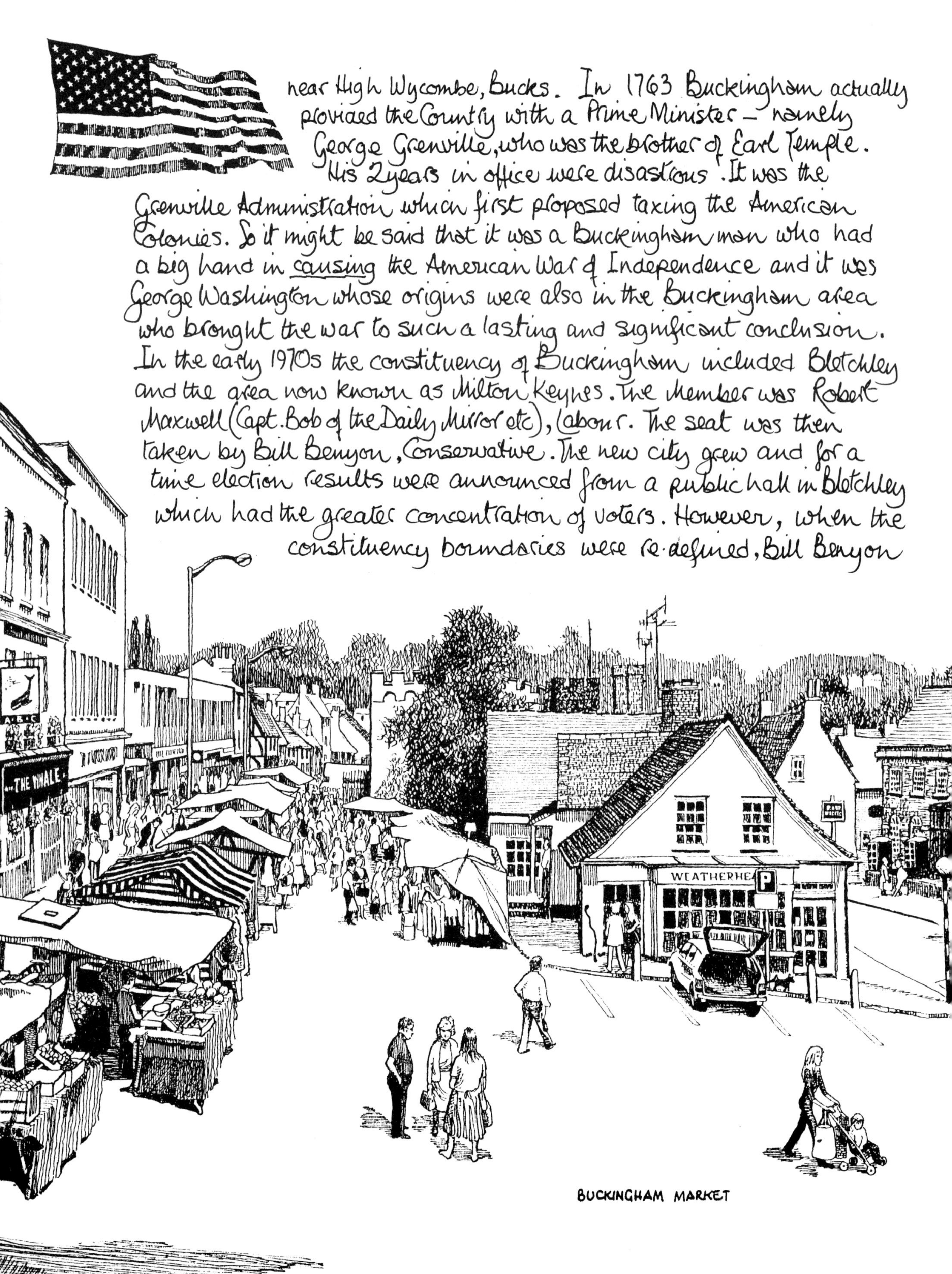

BUCKINGHAM MARKET

THE BULL RING SHOPS PRE-DATE BUCKINGHAM'S GREAT FIRE OF 1725. FOR MANY YEARS THEY WERE A COTTAGE WITH CYCLE & BARBER SHOPS ATTACHED, THEY ALSO SERVED AS THE TOWN'S HOT BATHS.

took the new seat of Milton Keynes; so Buckingham became the centre of a constituency again, this time covering Wolverton, Stony Stratford, Winslow, Pitstone and Haddenham. The Buckingham seat was won by George Walden, Conservative, who had previously been a diplomat with especial interests in Chinese & Russian affairs. Sarah Walden, his wife, is an art historian and one of Britain's foremost picture restorers. She is a conservation consultant and among her various notable clients is the Louvre. Sarah Walden's book "The Ravished Image – Or How to Ruin Masterpieces By Restoration", published in 1985, argues for a much restrained and more sympathetic approach to the cleaning and restoration of paintings. She is currently working on the story of Whistler's Mother.

A SQUARE BECAME A ROUNDABOUT A RING BECAME A SQUARE

The Market Square ceased to be looked upon as the centre of the Town some time in the 1950s. Now the Bull Ring is regarded as the centre. Some newcomers call it The Square because it is, and Market Hill, which runs across the top of it, houses the Tuesday and Saturday markets. These quiet little retail markets have their origins in the old livestock markets which dated from the fifteenth century and even earlier, and continued well into the twentieth. There are farmers around still, who remember the droving of stock to Buckingham Market.

I put together these pages about the market on a Tuesday in 1988, and while shopping in the morning I counted the stalls: there were two selling fish, three fruit and vegetables, four clothes including one specialising in Pakistani anoraks, two selling fabrics, one haberdashery, one cheese and bacon, one bread, one herbs & whole foods, one pet foods, one cut flowers, one potted plants and one hardware. On a Saturday there are additionally one more plant stall, a flower stall, a junk & secondhand bookstall, and the very popular stall of the Women's Institute with its free-range eggs and home-made cakes & cookies.

Also on a Saturday, for a short while early on, there is a line-up of Plymouth Brethren; shoppers seem to pass them at the trot, anxious to buy some eggs before they are all gone, oblivious to their testimonies and cries to return to the ways of the Lord, keen to return home to breakfast.

Now, the nearest livestock market is at Winslow — 5 miles away; 20 miles away is the Banbury livestock market which is said to have the largest throughput in the Country — maybe in Europe.

Some of Buckingham's market stalls are still laid out on long hand-barrows with wooden spoked wheels, and on non-market days they are stored behind the Whale public house. Half-way up Market Hill, The Whale is well

THE WHALE, ONCE ANDERSON'S HOTEL

situated and popular with the traders for whom there is a market day extension to drinking hours. It came into being in about 1839 and was known first as Anderson's Hotel.

The Old Gaol was built in 1748 and was part of a wider scheme to reclaim Buckingham's rightful status as County Town; but for most of its life it has been the Town's principal white elephant. Originally it was as square as a plywood fort for tin soldiers, and although it had 13 cells they were seldom, if ever, all in use. Security was poor and there are records of one prisoner letting himself down from the battlements and of another chap who walked out through the front door when no one was looking. The addition of the rounded front to provide quarters for the superintendent was made in 1839, and in certain sunlight its crumbling yellow stone looks like short cake, which contributes to its story-book appearance. At one time it housed the police office, and at another the Town fire engine. Larry the Lamb and Mr Grouser were seldom far away. In more recent years it has been used as a café and as an antique mart.

THE OLD GAOL 1981

In 1974, local government re-organisation required the Town to assign its Old Gaol to the careless hands of Aylesbury Vale Council (the Old Town Hall and Castle House were also part of the dowry); after witnessing the fate of the Old Town Hall, a group of Buckingham patriots formed the Heritage Trust. They retrieved the Old Gaol and raised enough money to carry out restoration work with the intention now of converting it into a museum and art gallery

Across the road from the Old Gaol is the King's Head pub which, until 1929, adjoined the Old Market House. Its former premises were demolished to provide a more spacious entry into the Town for the Maids Moreton Road. The Kings Head is a popular pub not least because of its landlord Van Marks and his wife Alice. Before they retired in 1988 they were the longest established publicans in the Town.

VAN MARKS OF COUNTY DOWN, LANDLORD OF THE KINGS HEAD FROM 1966 TO 1988

Behind the King's Head is the Salvation Army Hall, and it was somewhere beside this building that a schoolmaster was pilloried in the last century; pupils of his school were given leave to jeer and to lob what came to hand at their teacher, who had been found guilty of committing an act of indecency.

THE OLD MARKET HOUSE ONCE THE TALBOT INN ALSO KNOWN AS THE DOG.

Across the Maids Moreton Road is the Old Market House: it is said to date from the fifteenth century and was probably a merchant's house which later became used as a meeting place for those on business in

the Town at market time. In the basement there is still a cock fighting pit, although I gather it is now bricked-up. In this century Market House has been used as a restaurant and is said to be haunted by a Quaker Lady. There was a

PHANTOM CAPERS

Friends' Meeting House not far away – the building is still there, behind a house in the same terrace. It is said the Lady has a sense of humour, for she has been known to bring a waiter running by sounding the cow-bell at the serving hatch, or to shock a lone customer by drawing-up a chair to sit at the same table. She is often heard climbing the stairs or walking the landing but her speciality is to cause new waiters to wet their trouser legs when she taps them on the shoulders in the Gents.

From here on the road is known as the High Street leading to the part of Buckingham known as North End. Peter Hain who has lived around Buckingham much of his life, is a great story teller. This little ditty of his is about the people who lived in North End:

PETER HAIN

Down North End where the World first began,
Lives old Spencer and old Black Fan,
Mrs Stratton slim and slender,
Mrs. Capel the britches mender,
Mr. Perfect who keeps the peace,
And wicked Bill who defies the Police.

Peter was born very early on this century and has had a variety of jobs: for some time he was the driver of a steam roller, and during the Second World War he served as some kind of peripatetic batman. Amongst those who benefited from his services were King Christian of Denmark and Douglas Fairbanks. Peter is well known as a conversationalist at almost every watering hole in Buckingham and the villages – he is happy to chat to almost anyone he meets but, as he puts it, "I like the old country ways and sometimes I'm mistaken for a tramp – I'm not, but some of the new people don't understand".

DICK MAY, POSTMAN MARKET HILL AND NORTH END.

If on a summer's evening, you stop for a drink at a village pub and watch a group of Morris Dancers, there is usually a little chap dressed up as the Fool – he will be prancing around, hitting people on the head with his inflated pig's bladder. Despite his advanced years this will probably be Peter Hain.

A·ROUND·&·A·BOUT·WITH·A·CURATE

When the fun-fair visits the Town (its Charter dates from 1554) there are stalls, caravans, merry-go-rounds, dodgems and big wheels occupying every available patch of tarmac from the Old Town Hall to as far as North End. For many years the boxing booth was one of the great attractions and this was usually set-up on level ground at North End. Prize money would entice local lads to try their luck in the ring, against the Fun Fair's own hardened fighters, who were sufficiently experienced to cope with most contenders. The lads of the early 1950s are now about 60 years old and some recall the time the curate of Maids Moreton first appeared in the crowd to take up the challenge. He strode forward, threw off his cape and was ready dressed for a bout in the ring. What was not generally known at first was that the curate was a boxer of some accomplishment. He won with a knock-out in the 3rd round and was so concerned about his opponent, who seemed in no hurry to pick himself up, that he helped bring him round and insisted on giving him his own winnings. The curate made a star appearance at the boxing booth each year for sometime, and usually succeeded in bringing the match to a conclusion in the 3rd round.

At one time the High Street and North End must have been chock-a-block with pubs. There was the 16th Angel which closed in 1938, The Black Swan of the 19th, The Boar's Head which lasted for only 16 years in the 17th, the Cock Inn 16th to 19th, The Dog which opened in the 17th, changed its name to the Talbot and closed in 1751, the 18th Fox and Hounds, which later became known as the Hare and Hounds, then closed in 1929, the 18th Horse & Groom which still has its name displayed but which closed in 1963, the 18th Trooper which packed up in 1907 and the 17th Ship Inn, now known as the Grand Junction Inn and the only pub left in the whole of the High Street and North End. The landlord is Ian Price, who also has the job of Town Crier for Buckingham.

The Town Crier is not elected, but the Town Mayor is, first as a Town Councillor, then by a vote in the Council Chamber. How long the Mayor should stay in Office is often a matter of lively debate for

IAN PRICE
TOWN CRIER

there are some who would parade in the mayoral robes unto death, whilst others give the post their vigorous enthusiasm for one two or three years before returning full-time to their own busy and successful careers. Among mayors in this category was David Stevens.

David is a landscape designer of some distinction: the RHS awarded him Gold Medals 4 years out of the last 5 for his garden designs at the Chelsea Flower Show. I have had the pleasure of illustrating, in watercolour, two of David's books and have also had the unusual task this year of producing a landscape painting based upon his proposed design & planting schedules for the next Chelsea Flower Show. (After years of producing pictures of what I see before me, it is strange to paint a landscape which has not yet come about). A television programme of David Stevens' work called 'Reflections of Gold' was broadcast in May 1988.

Buckingham and its villages have quite a number of accomplished gardeners: there is Doug Warr of Steeple Claydon whose chrysanthemums have been shown since 1963 and, to date, have won him 41 silver medals (5 at national level) 14 bronze and 9 of the 'Banksian' medals. Also, there is Eric Fern who has a beautiful and extraordinary garden of coniferous trees and shrubs. Mr & Mrs Fern moved to Addington Road, Buckingham in the first year of their marriage over 50 years ago and Mrs Fern's family pulled her leg because of the anniversary present she had chosen for her husband; it was an envelope containing just two seeds. They were the seeds of an Atlantic Cedar. Eric planted them both and one now stands at the rear of the house — towering above it; the other was cultivated as a Bonsai. Since then it has been Eric's practice to plant 2 at a time, keeping one as a potted dwarf. Their little garden is a joy to see — if fortune had given them a stately home their garden would have world renown.

ERIC FERN

One of the more curious little corners of the Town is the Chewar. It is an alley-way which runs from close-by Cannon Corner, passes the back doors of Lloyds Bank and W.H. Smith's, then emerges near the top of Market Hill. For many years the local explanation for such an unusual name was that 'Chewar' was derived from 'sewer', because the present passageway is said to follow the route of a drain which once ran from 'The Shambles' (now Barclays Bank). In the nineteenth century 'The Shambles' was a complex of stalls overlooking the Bull Ring, and one of the stalls was a butcher's where beasts would be led from the livestock market, slaughtered and jointed there and then, and sold for local consumption. So, such premises would certainly have needed a drain, but a brief look at the lie-of-the-land shows that a sewer with that route would be flowing up-hill. How such an explanation could have been told and

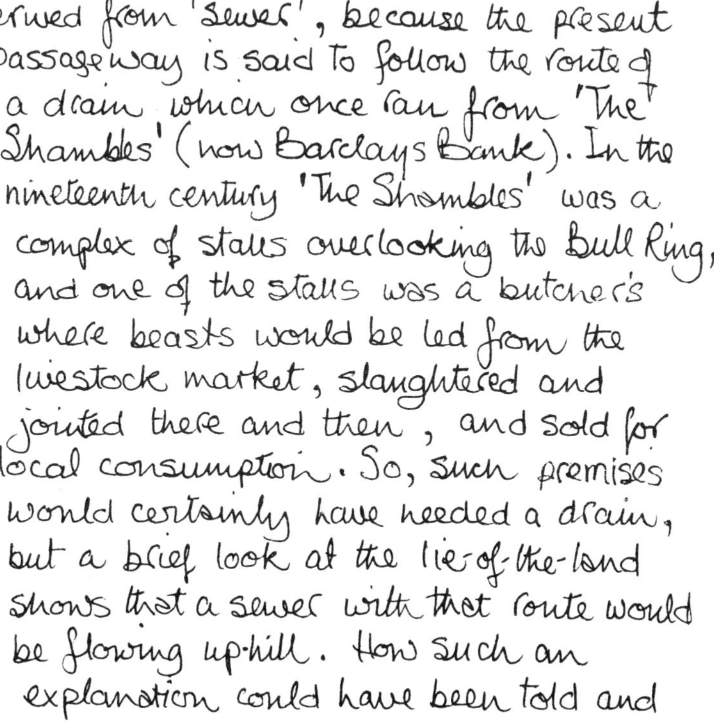

THE START OF THE CHEWAR

BUCKINGHAM BOOKSHOP

re-told for so long I cannot imagine. Another explanation occurred to me when I first came across the place: a 'chewer' (pronounced chewah in the nineteenth century) was a member of the household of Coptic gentry. Below the position of nanny but above that of nursery-maid, she was employed especially for masticating food, which she would spoon from her own mouth to her infant charges', thus improving their digestion. Such a lady might well have arrived in the Town during the last century as part of the retinue of some visiting family of note. During her stay she could well have been dismissed for becoming tired, slothful or even toothless, and feeling totally at home in Buckingham, settled in a cottage in the lane now named after her profession and which for many years was a useful shortcut from an off--licence to the Town's bookshop.

I discarded this explanation when I discovered 'The Tchure' at Deddington; there, its function is clearer. A tchure or chewer is to do with the corralling of beasts; it funnels animals from their lairage into the market pens or place of slaughter.

The Buckingham Bookshop on Market Hill is owned and run by David Clegg who in 1985 surprised the Town when he disclosed that he had received an invitation to attend the royal wedding of Prince Andrew and Miss Sarah Ferguson; David, who had been at school and Sandhurst with Major Ferguson, is the godfather of the Duchess of York.

Earlier in its life, the Buckingham Bookshop was the office of the

Town's newspaper — the Buckingham Advertiser — launched in 1853. If you look carefully at the skylight above the bookshop door the name can still be read.

Vic Tattersall, a name much respected amongst journalists, was 'The Advertiser's' editor from 1967 until 1987. Vic had an unusual start in life. The Tattersall family was originally from Yorkshire, and his grandfather and father had established a flourishing publishing business in England and Germany. Vic was sent by his father to be educated in Germany with the intention that one day Vic would join the family firm. In England Vic attended a school where the boys were expected to join the Scouts. However, when Hitler became Chancellor in Germany, the International Scout Movement was banned there and membership of the Hitler Youth became compulsory for all boys, including Vic. Once, when Hitler made a visit to Weimar near the school, the Young Englander was required to take part in a parade, and narrowly missed having to shake hands with the Führer. Vic Tattersall was brought home in good time for the outbreak of hostilities, and he gave no one any doubt about his loyalties; he served in the Royal Navy, first in the North Atlantic and later in the Mediterranean. By the end of the war he was minesweeping the North Sea and was one of the youngest in the Royal Navy to be given his own command. After the war he did a bit of farming and wrote a column for the County

VIC TATTERSALL EDITOR OF THE TOWN'S NEWSPAPER FROM 1967 UNTIL 1987

PRINTERS' MEWS
OR FLEECE YARD

paper, the Bucks Herald, which was the start of his distinguished career in local journalism.

When the Advertiser occupied the premises on Market Hill the paper was printed 'out the back'. Vehicular access to the printing works was through what is commonly known as Printers' Mews, which the local authority, based in Aylesbury, insists should be called Fleece Yard. Amongst the various enterprises now run from Printers' Mews is the Buckingham Movie Museum — home of the John Burgoyne-Johnson collection of film projectors and movie cameras, some dating from before 1912, when Charles Pathé first made movies with the revolutionary new Pathéscope Safety Film. The Movie Museum also contains its own fully equipped little theatre.

The Town's cinema in Chandos Road, which was finally closed in 1987, is said to occupy the site of an old theatre 'in the round' constructed of timber; now it is used for car sales.

FROM LETTERPRESS TO LITHOGRAPHY WITH AN ORATORIO

Printers' Mews continues to have connections with the printing trade. A small typesetting and printing business occupies premises there, and it is run by Bruce Kershaw, who is more widely known as a singer. Bruce is a bass-baritone. During his days at Trinity College of Music he was granted a scholarship to attend Aldeburgh to study under Lord (Benjamin) Britten and Sir Peter Pears. In 1977 Bruce was invited to tour with Kent Opera and in 1978 he gave his first notable solo when he was invited to take the baritone role in Elgar's Coronation Ode at the Royal Silver Jubilee Gala Concert in the Royal Albert Hall. He was accompanied by the combined bands of the Guards, the Royal Marines and the Royal Air Force, and it is some measure of Bruce Kershaw's voice to know that he managed without amplification. Since then Bruce has continued to be in demand as a soloist; he took part in a special performance of The Vespers by Claudio Monteverdi given before Her Majesty the Queen at St. James's Palace, and he is a regular singer at St. Margaret's, Westminster, the Parish Church of the House of Commons.

BRUCE KERSHAW

† Most of the tone drawings in this book, including this one of Bruce Kershaw, were carried out with common Bic ballpens (the slim yellow ones, which produce a fine black line and are only a few pence to buy). It is my experience that the first ½" of use is too pale, so I start by using them for writing; then when they are flowing well, I use them for drawing — cleaning the tips continually with a tissue for they are inclined to blob. The final inch flows too freely and blobs all the time, so they are generally relegated to a writing job. At its best the Bic is a remarkably sensitive pen, fine for features. But sometimes it is too fine for reproduction; in the drawing of Ian Price on page 79 I used firm lines throughout, so the plate maker could produce a film directly from it, but the rest (mainly of heads) are too fine so first they had to be 'shot' through a fine screen: thus they appear to be composed of a stipple, a process more commonly used in the printing

of photographs. The disadvantage of a ball-pen is that it cannot be erased; you must hope to be correct first time, or start again. +

The Old Latin School, Buckingham

This little building started life some eight hundred years ago and was used first as an hospital, later as a chantry; then with an endowment from Edward VI in 1548 it became a grammar school. In the 17th century a master's house was built at the rear and the chantry remained a boarding grammar school until 1908 when the Royal Latin School, as it became known, moved to new premises in Chandos Road. The move in 1908 was not a smooth one. There was no accommodation for boarders at the new premises and for the first time in its history the school was obliged to take girls; headmaster Matthew Cox refused to move so a new head was appointed. In the late 1930s H.B. Toft, who captained England Rugby, was headmaster of the 'Latin'. During the 2nd World War the Maths & Physics master - Tommy Allitt ran the Town's Air Training Squadron from the school; now like Mr Chips he has retired and lives in a house overlooking the school's old wrought iron gates which bear the initials RLS. In 1966 the school moved again, and once more it took on boarders; in the 1970s it survived the enthusiasm for comprehensive education and today it is one of the few remaining 'selective' grammar schools. Since 1972 Patti Pearce has been head of art at the RLS. Earlier in her career she founded an art department in a bush school in Kenya; more recently her floral paintings and her Tolkien type landscapes have charmed thousands.

PATTI PEARCE

This drawing (with apologies to VanDyke) was produced to advertise a mock battle at Finmere by the Sealed Knot. In reality there were no great Civil War battles fought in the immediate vicinity of Buckingham, but some of the surrounding villages did suffer from "manor house skirmishes" and the accompanying hooliganism of the time. However, Buckingham did witness some of the comings & goings: it is said that Parliamentary troops were billeted at the White Swan – now the 'Swan & Castle' – and in the loft above the 'Cromwell Room' there are still bunks with racks for muskets. On 22nd June 1644 King Charles I marched to Buckingham with 9000 foot & 3000 horse and remained in the Town for four days. The King is said to have lodged at Castle House, which is also said to have given shelter to Catherine of Aragon during her marriage

The Swan & Castle Hotel, Buckingham.

CASTLE HOUSE

to King Henry VIII. In 1708 it was given a new facade, and during the nineteenth century Castle House was a bank and was called The House of Lombard. The broad stretch of road infront of Castle House was the Horse Fair, in the centre of which was the Market Cross. The base of the cross is in the old church yard in Hunter Street — the top is said to be in a private garden in Gawcott..

CHANGING USES

On the other side of Horse Fair and next door to the Barrel public house (earlier named the Kings Arms) stood The Swan Brewery. It was the property of the Dukes of Buckingham. In the middle of the last century the annual rent was £60 and each year the brewer was expected to produce not less than 266 hogsheads of ale, beer & porter. Now the property is a garage

THE OLD SCHOOL
SCHOOL LANE

Next door is Chandos House, once a private dwelling, now the offices of an electrical components firm. Here the ghost of an attractive lady patrols the front wall on certain dates each year and more than once is said to have delighted those leaving the Barrel at closing time.

School Lane, as it is known, once had two schools. Both buildings still

N° 62 NELSON STREET IN 1923.

stand but both have changed their uses; this one, the Old School, was converted to a private house in the early 1980s.

My drawing of Woottons the Bakers of Nelson Street (1923) was commissioned by two descendants of the gentleman standing at the door. They lent me family photographs from which to work and it surprised me how much information can be obtained from old photographs if they are in focus. Later I made this quick sketch of the shop as it is now; a fishing tackle shop with tax consultants above. When the modernisation took place I do not know.

N° 62 NELSON STREET

TO THE GLORY OF GOD AND IN GRATEFUL MEMORY OUR GLORIOUS DEAD. 1914 – 1918

ADAMS HARRY	CLIFFORD SAM	HOLTON E.J. SGT. MM.	PICKERING FRED	SWIFT G. CPL
ATLAY A.C. SGT	COOK A. CPL	HUTT W.J. LCE CPL	PICKERING WILLIAM H.	TAYLOR WILLIAM
BANDY J.T. CO.SGT MAJ.	COOK WILLIAM A.	JEFFREY GEORGE H	PRIEST H.A. CAPT RNVR.	THORPE A. LCE CPL
BENNETT C.H. CAPT M.C.	CROOK ERNEST	JEFFREY J. SGT	PURCELL REGINALD J.H.	TOMPKINS JOSEPH
BENNETT WILLIAM G.	DILLOW EDWARD T.	JERRAMS JOHN E	READ R. SGT MAJ.	TOMPKINS W.G. SGT
BEX PHILLIP F.	DUNKLEY CHARLES	JONES HENRY	READ FRED	TYRELL FRED
BOND JAMES R.	DUNKLEY F. SGT	JONES T.B. SGT	RIDGWAY H.J. SGT MAJ.	TYRELL WALTER J.
BROCK THOMAS	DUNKLEY J.G. CPL	JUDD G.C. SGT	ROADS HARRY	WATTS FRANCIS T.
BULL ALFRED	ERBACH FREDERICK W.	MAKEPEACE TOM. F.	SHEDD PERCY J.	WATTS H.E. CPL
BULL R.E.B. LIEUT	FRANKLIN JAMES	MARSH ALFRED J.	SHEDD FRANK H.	WATSON P. LCE CPL
BURROWS ARTHUR T	GARDNER C.V. CAPT	MARSHALL J.T. REG.SGT MAJ.	SHERGOLD G.F. LCE CPL	WESTLEY CLARENCE H.
BURROWS ALBERT	GARDNER PERCY	MEADS ALBERT T.	SMITH GEORGE E	WHITE CHARLES
BURROWS WILLIAM J.T.	GAUNT PERCY	MEADS E. CPL	SMITH GERALD O.	WHITE GEORGE T.
BURGESS HARRY	GRIFFIN WILLIAM	MEADS WILLIAM	SMITH M.J. CPL	WHITEHEAD GEORGE
BUTLER THOMAS W	HARRIS JIM	MELLISS A.D.J. LIEUT	SOTON RICHARD	WILLIAMS REGINALD J.
BUNKER PERCY	HARTLAND H. DOUGLAS	MOBBS FREDERICK G.	SOTON WILL	WINSOR GEORGE A.
CHURCH REGINALD G	HEALEY EDWARD J.	MORGANS T. 2nd LIEUT	STAPLETON W.G. LCE CPL	WINTERBURN GEORGE A
CHURCH STANLEY	HENLEY J. LCE CPL	PAINTER ARTHUR H.	STOKES HAROLD E.	WISE GEORGE
CLARKE S. LCE CPL	HICKS FREDERICK	PAINTER WILL	STURGESS ALBERT.	WATTS SAMUEL.

THEIR NAMES SHALL LIVE FOR EVERMORE. 1939 – 1945

ACHERMAN L.	CAWSE N.	HARRIS R.W.	RICHARDSON C.G.	SIMMONDS A.E.
BAKER A.H.	COX M.C.	HOUNSLOW J.	RICHARDSON J.H.	SMITH P.T.
BAUCHAN R.L.	DAGLEY E.	JARVIS F.W.	RIDLEY F.P.	THOMAS H.G.
BISHOP R.E	DILLOW W.T	JONES G.W	SAXBY F.	VALENTINE G.A.
BURCHETT G.D.	HARRIS D.W.	PAYNE G.F.	SEARS A.J.	

The memorial to the dead of two world wars stands a few yards to the north of the Parish Church. 95 Buckingham men were killed in the First War, 24 in the Second. Many of the family names are in the Town today.

At some time in its life this attractive coachhouse and stables (built 1875) served as the Town's fire station. Adjoining it is a matching gateway and balcony to No 11 Castle Hill. It is an unusually ornamental building and visitors often stop to stare and wonder. It has decorative ridge tiles and fancy iron work on the front gable – a hipped gable at the rear; the hay loft is timber framed with panels of incised rendering; it has patterned bricks and carved lintels and from every aspect you can see the symbol of the Aesthetic Movement – the Sunflower. 'The Coach House' was designed by Edward Swinfen Harris (1841 – 1924); he worked in London early on, then in Stony Stratford around which much of his work can be seen. Fascinated by the styles and ornament of mediaeval architecture, he toured Europe

THE COACH HOUSE AT THE GATEWAY TO THE PARISH CHURCH OF St PETER & St PAUL

with a sketchbook in 1882, then returned to design more of his own well-ornamented buildings for north Buckinghamshire. He built a house for himself, in the High Street of Stony Stratford, and named it Rothenburg after the town in Germany where the architecture most impressed him. The house is now owned & occupied by the architect & historian Mr. C.T.P. Woodfield who has studied the work of ESH and who kindly gave me access to his notes. Some builders found Swinfen Harris difficult to work with, and I am told there were others who refused to work with him a second time. If Swinfen Harris had a weakness it was that sometimes he may have allowed aesthetic considerations to override practicalities. His Doctor's House at Stony is a fine one but, because of the position of the archway, the coach house was said to be almost impossible to use. The Old School at Addington has a roof which was not designed to accommodate a battery of chimneys, and some of the internal doors were planned with insufficient space to open fully.

Nevertheless, it is an attractive piece of architecture considered the finest example of his work. Now it has been converted into a house, owned and occupied by Frank Kay (F.X. Kay) who is one of Britain's independent inventors. It was one of Frank's ancestors who was responsible for the 'flying shuttle' which started Britain weaving at such a pace it might be said to have triggered the Industrial Revolution. His father designed the breech of the Vickers gun, and Frank is responsible for many of the advances in pneumatics – his reputation & patents are world wide, and in the industry he is known as the Einstein of Pneumatics.

F.X.KAY

At the southern access to the church are these houses – built in 1836. Buckingham had more than one serious fire but the worst was in 1725. It started somewhere in Nelson Street and swept through this part of the Town

CHURCH STREET

St RUMBOLD'S LANE

138 houses were burnt out and over 500 people were made homeless (more than 1/3 of the population then) The fire also put an end to Buckingham's hopes of retaining its status as County Town. It was a depressed and demoralised place; there are reports that many of the buildings were not restored some 50 years later, and in some cases townspeople were still camping out in the shells of their former family homes. One small piece of carved timber on the corner of a house in St Rumbold's Lane gives some indication of the type of building which existed there before.

St Rumbold was of royal birth and was baptised at Kings Sutton in the seventh century. According to legend he spoke a few holy words then died, an infant. He was buried at Kings Sutton; subsequently his body was moved to Brackley and finally to Buckingham where a shrine was established, but this disappeared during the reign of Henry VIII. St Rumbold's spring is said to be near the Prince of Prussia public house (re-named The Britannia after 1914). Until 1923 no one knew the whereabouts of the font associated with the baptism of St. Rumbold. But during a gale the spire of the Parish Church of Kings Sutton was blown down, and after its restoration, the vicar ordered a general tidy-up of the church yard, including the removal of an old mound situated close to where the spire had fallen —

THE SAXON FONT AT THE PARISH CHURCH IN KINGS SUTTON.

— the mound had been there for as long as anyone could remember and no one had ever been sufficiently curious to find out what it contained. However, when it was opened up it revealed — a Saxon font.

TWISTED CHIMNEYS

Browne Willis, the Town's eighteenth century historian, believed that Buckingham benefitted in no small way from the legend & the shrine; we can thank St Rumbold for several of the Town's inns & taverns which might well have been established originally to cater for the pilgrims.

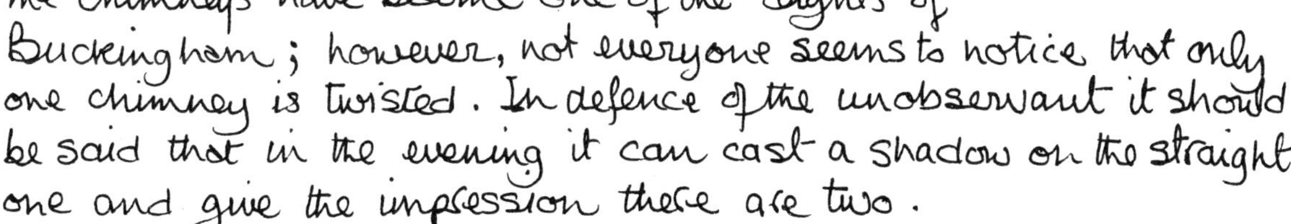

The house known as Twisted Chimneys (a word so easily misspelt) is attached to Buckingham Manor. The chimneys have become one of the Sights of Buckingham; however, not everyone seems to notice that only one chimney is twisted. In defence of the unobservant it should be said that in the evening it can cast a shadow on the straight one and give the impression there are two.

Well Street leads from Church Street, back towards the Town centre, following the curve of the eastern ramparts of the castle. My drawing here is of the rear of N°54; timber framed and panelled by wattle and daub. One has the feeling it is held erect by the stone chimney stack, which looks as though it was made for a larger building. To the right is the wooden cross of Well Street (non-conformist) Church, redesigned in 1987 by Buckingham architect Peter Bradley. Above is the spire of the Parish Church.

N°54

WELL STREET WAS ONCE A BUSY STREET OF LOCAL SHOPS - GROCERS FISHSHOPS, COBBLERS, DAIRIES, ...

THE WOOLPACK INN

In 1577 there were 14 licensed houses within the borough. By 1839 it had risen to 31; now there are 11 pubs and a handful of restaurants with wine licenses. The Woolpack Inn in Well Street has served beer for most of those years. Timbers on the upper floors show that the Woolpack was originally of cruck construction, which must make it a good contender for one of the Town's oldest pubs. In 1574 the Woolpack was leased to Katherine Agard for a term of 2000 years at an annual rent of 2d. Alas, poor Katherine did not last the course, otherwise beer might be a little cheaper today. In 1694 the Inn was kept by another lady whose son worked in the Town as a tanner. In the nineteenth century the Woolpack was frequented by farmers and dealers, especially on Mondays, when a sheep & calf market was held in Well Street — the pens were erected in the road against the raised pavement opposite. At one time the Woolpack was granted its own fair called 'Ann North's Fair' after the landlady of the time and this was held on each 'old New Years Day'.

LEGAL MEASURE

TWO PINTS —— ONE QUART
FOUR QUARTS —— ONE GALLON
ONE GALLON —— ONE ARGUMENT
ONE ARGUMENT —— ONE POLICEMAN
ONE POLICEMAN —— ONE SUMMONS

ONE MAGISTRATE, ONE POLICEMAN, ONE CLERK —— 20/- or 14 DAYS

MORAL

COME HERE AND GET THE BEST OF BEER
DON'T LET THE BEER GET THE BEST OF YOU.

When Peter Steers ran the pub in the 1970s this notice was displayed in the public bar. Peter was a particularly fine cook and he had another finely developed ability: he would make customers feel either very welcome, or definitely not. Also, if you

Nº 59 WELL St.

wished to be professionally insulted there was nowhere better in the Town than the Woolpack Inn. I was amongst a select group which was regularly insulted several times a week.

Many of the houses in Well Street are listed, by English Heritage, as historic buildings, and when the Town was designated a 'conservation area' the grading of each property rose. These Georgian houses rose from III to II.

Nº 60 WELL St.

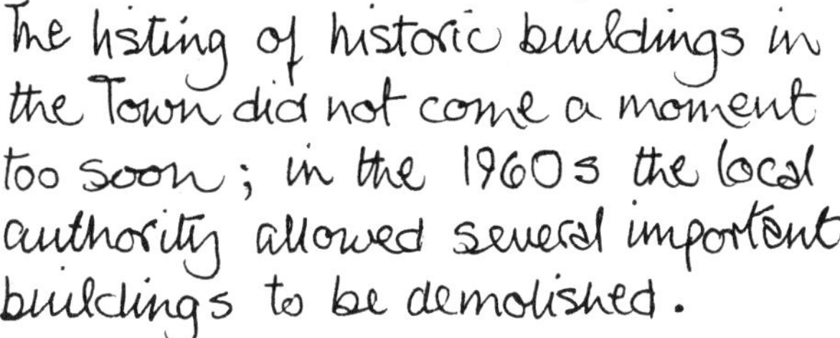

The listing of historic buildings in the Town did not come a moment too soon; in the 1960s the local authority allowed several important buildings to be demolished.

Running parallel with the stripped pine industry of the 1970s & 80s has been the cottage industry of 'doing-up' houses. Some of the listed buildings in the Town have received a thorough gutting by their temporary owners, had all antiquity removed, and then been totally rebuilt. Outside,

Nºs 5 & 4 WELL St.

they are facsimiles of what was there before, or have become someone's romantic idea of what they should be like; inside, they now have the sharp slick rectangularity of modern houses.

WELL STRE GARAGE

Further along Well Street is Davey Bros.. Their garage occupies what was once the Old Meeting House. Previously it had been an orphanage for boys.

One of Terry Davey's delights is racing cars like these, and for two years running, he was Class 10 Champion of Thames Valley. His brother Bob 'invented' the electric clock; disappointed to find he had been beaten to it he sometimes turns his back upon the World — rather as I have drawn him here. When he first saw this drawing he said "Oh no! look what he's gone and done. He's gone and bloody drawn me!"

Behind, and next door to the White Hart Hotel is a yellow brick building known to older Buckingham people as Holland's Follie. The building is referred to in the writings of Flora Thompson: her uncle Recab Holland lived there and ran a cobbling business from it; in "Over to Candleford" he is "Uncle Tom". In the last century it had been Mr Holland's intention, or maybe his father's, to cash-in on the proximity of Northampton's flourishing shoe trade. The yellow brick building was to house new shoe-making machinery but, when it was completed, the machinery was found to be too heavy or too large for the structure so the enterprise was abandoned. During the Second World War it became a cosmetics factory for Goya. More recently it was used by Markham's the ironmongers. The latest plans are to convert it into flats.

HOLLAND'S FOLLY

† When drawing high buildings close to, like the one of Well Street Garage, the convergence of vertical lines is important. Until you can imagine the position of the zenith it is worth using a piece of 8ft beading bought from a DIY shop. After making rough sketches of proportions and alignment and taking note of disappearing points, a fresh start can be made in the studio, securing the beading with an elastic band to the upright of a chair placed beyond the drawing board at an appropriate distance. There is no need to be precise, as a draughtsman; a simple fan of faint pencil strokes is enough to keep the drawing on the right lines. †

One of Bertie Clarke's many jobs during a lifetime in Buckingham and around, was at the counter of Markhams the ironmongers or out-the-back dispensing paraffin.

BERTIE CLARKE

BRIDGE STREET

Markhams remained defiantly unmerchandised to the day it closed in 1987. The front-shop had a sturdy counter which was approached across well-worn floorboards; from floor to ceiling there were wooden drawers and secured to the front of each was a sample of the kind of thing it contained – a brass door knob, a fencing staple, a gate hinge, a castor wheel, a pair of scissors, a grummet, a six-inch screw. If you asked for something unusual or bulky you might be invited out-the-back into Holland's Folly, which was a treasury of plumbing joints, agricultural hand tools, hose pipes, wheel-barrows and a thousand other things all placed, without a sign of fancy packaging, on solid benches or shelves, or strung from ceiling hooks. There was a comprehensive stock of glass shades and cylinders for oil lamps, and one day when I went to buy a new handle for a pick-axe I saw, hanging in an obscure corner, a ring door handle with its ornamental back plate – waiting for the day someone might build a new Gothic church.

Bertie Clarke's first job when he left school was on a farm – "I went to work for a woman near Gawcott. On the first morning she

SNAPPER.

gave me an iron file and sent me into a cowshed to get rid of the wrinkles in the horns of the cattle, so that when they went to market the buyers mightn't notice how old they were." A pint of bitter, a rum chaser and a game of dominoes on the table before him, Bertie could not now be happier. "The best place I ever worked was at Mr. Markham's. Now he's what I call a gentleman."

In the early 1970s Markham's was not the only shop resisting modern retail marketing. There was an unpretentious little shop in the Market Square with a range of cigarettes and snuff of which any West End tobacconist might be proud. One clothing shop, with many rooms on different levels, sold their socks from brown cardboard boxes on the floor, petticoats and pairs of long drawers were heaped on trestle tables, and brassieres were hung upon the wall like canvas buckets. Until 1980 Clay's the Butchers slaughtered animals, enough for their 30 branches, behind their shop beside the Old Gaol; new comers from urban areas were sometimes quite upset.

LOITERING WITH INTENT

In the 1980s 'Snapper', the Jack Russell I've drawn above, lived in Chandos Road, and each day he would make his way into the Town to do his round of the butchers' shops. Sometimes he was lucky enough to be given a bone, almost as big as himself. However, Snapper did not always have the patience to wait for generosity, and sometimes he would feel the need to help himself. I witnessed his arrest on one occasion; he was handed over like a parcel, feet uppermost, to a policeman with a waiting squad car. Sid Vicious, despite his name, is a more orderly animal-about-town; resident of the Red Cross Centre, he is a part-time assistant in the public library.

SID VICIOUS

Buckingham's public library receives a steady flow of work from local authors — people who have written of their villages or families, or of the area during Edwardian times. Of the Town itself there have been several books. In 1984, The Book of Buckingham, a history by professional historian Dr John Clarke, was published by Barracuda Books. One author who lives locally, is Laurie Graham — her book 'The Parents' Survival Guide' was read on BBC Radio 4 in 1987. However, the area seems to have bred or attracted more artists than authors. Artist Norman Tennant, born in 1896, lived at Drayton Parslow; he wrote and illustrated 'A Saturday Night Soldier's War' published by The Kylin Press. Now, we have Peter Newcombe who

THE PAINTERS

became more widely known when his work was used on a set of postage stamps — but his paintings of the Northamptonshire countryside were already hugely popular — so too is Dennis Rothwell Bailey's work, which is sought by many galleries. Robert Read's paintings of the Buckinghamshire countryside are also very popular for they seem to have the lighting and some of the loose informality which first attracted people to the work of Cotman, Crome & Bright. Paintings by Diana Winkfield are much published and her work is regularly exhibited at Liberty's gallery. The exquisite little still life paintings, by Sue Read, brought about her election to the Royal Institute of Painters in Watercolour in 1985; she is one of the select group of just 10 ladies out of a total membership of about 60 at the present time. Then there is Edward Stamp R.I. whose paintings of Buckinghamshire have made him one of the most popular landscape painters in Britain today.

There are many other painters in the Buckingham area and from time to time some get themselves into narrow scrapes. One man received a reprimand when he thought he could enhance his reputation by posting a piece of his work to St. James Palace, then claiming he had a painting in the Royal Collection. Another had a speculative career painting country houses, hoping to sell his efforts to the ladies within, who would peer at him from behind their curtains and sometimes ask him in for coffee; after years of successful practice and 'befriending' many of his lonely patrons, he was eventually persuaded to leave the area by a posse of enraged husbands.

One landscape painter of my acquaintance would set out on his day's work across the fields, carrying his drawing board with paper ready stretched, and a satchel containing his paints, sandwiches and a flask. Sometimes he would also take his gun and a dog. One day a farmer spotted feathers sprouting from the painter's bag and demanded the cost of the transgression — a good sized painting of his prize bull. This the painter provided — and a very good painting it was; the farmer was so pleased with it he gave the artist permission to shoot his land on a more regular basis.

There was one hapless man who exhibited a number of skilfully executed charcoal life drawings of his wife and ex-wife and managed to upset both ladies at once. Although they had given their approval for the drawings to be shown at an exhibition they appeared at the pre-view to be less than happy. The artist's wife was offended because the drawings of her were listed at a lower price than those of his ex-wife who, in turn, was annoyed because she believed he had shown greater consideration for the modesty of his new wife than he had for hers.

✢ He was not the first to become aware of the correlation between nudity & price. Clearly Russell Flint's paintings were valued with that principle in mind. The evidence might not have been so clear in the eighteenth century: perhaps Goya was uncertain about such matters when he produced clothed & nude versions of the same pictures (The Maja clothed, The Maja nude) and maybe they were an attempt by him to hedge his bets. On the other hand the gossip which began to grow soon after Goya's death, was that his model had been none other than the disreputable Duchess of Alba, with whom Goya is said to have had an affair. There was a limerick going the rounds at the time:

Said the Duchess of Alba to Goya,
'Remember that I'm your employer.'
So he painted her twice,
Once clothed to look nice,
And once in the nude
to annoy her.

A MASTER RESTORER

Arthur Clark is a restorer of old masters; his reputation extends beyond Britain and Europe into Asia, from where he receives invitations to stay for months at a time to restore the works of art in the great palaces of India. In between times he is back in England undertaking work at stately homes or on humbler family heirlooms belonging to the rest of us.

A TOUR OF THE VILLAGES

In 1985 I was asked to illustrate a calendar for the coming year; carelessly I chose as a subject the Village Greens of North Buckinghamshire, believing there would be plenty from which to choose. There needed to be seven drawings in all, and a village green was to be defined as an area of grass upon which there were a pump, a telephone box, possibly a war memorial, and around which there were gathered a church, a chapel, a pub and the village shop & post office. I was hard put to find even six in N. Bucks and seldom could I find more than 4 of the 8 elements in any one place. This had to be my seventh drawing.

THE VILLAGE GREEN FROM INSIDE THE GATES OF MENTMORE – A MAGNIFICENT HOUSE BUILT BY BARON de ROTHSCHILD IN 1851. SUBSEQUENTLY IT BECAME THE SEAT OF LORD ROSEBERY.

NOW THE OWNER IS THE 'WORLD GOVERNMENT OF THE AGE OF ENLIGHTENMENT' AND IT HOUSES THE MAHARISHI EUROPEAN RESEARCH UNIVERSITY.

GREAT NORWOOD.

BRILL NEAR THE OXFORDSHIRE BORDER

Most of the green at Great Horwood has become a gravel car park. William Warham, once vicar of Great Horwood became Archbishop of Canterbury and married Henry VIII to Catherine of Aragon.

One radio broadcaster was heard to explain to several million people that the name of the new city of Milton Keynes

THE VILLAGE OF MILTON KEYNES

was especially composed from the names of John Milton and Maynard Keynes, to represent the successful fusing of art & industry. However, the village of Milton Keynes was established long before either gentleman was born, and it was just one of the established communities which the new city consumed. For some people in north Bucks, Milton Keynes is another one of those 'hideous carbuncles', for others it is – a convenience.

THORNBOROUGH VILLAGE GREEN.

Of all the village greens in north Bucks, Thornborough's is the most complete. Above, you are looking at the Two Brewers public house, the village shop & post office, the cottage which once housed the village bobby, the Methodist Chapel, the entrance to the Manor, the Parish Church, the pond, and the village pound. The pump is outside what was once my house – the old Forge – only just in this picture, and if I had drawn more to the right you would see the telephone box. The Green itself is used for the village fête, an annual fun fair, and as the meet for the local fox hunt. The war memorial can be seen on the

THORNBOROUGH PARISH CHURCH

front wall in my drawing of the Parish Church, and to the right is the village hall. It may sound and seem to be an unchanging place but it isn't. It is said that in the 1940s & '50s Thornborough was 'rough' – a place for fights; in the '60s & '70s when I was there it was a place for practical jokes and hearty drinking; now it is a quiet dormitory – Milton Keynes is 20 minutes away, London just an hour or so.

Parts of Thornborough village were once owned by Magdalen College, and much of Padbury, not far away, was (and some still is) owned by All Souls. Many of the houses in Padbury are thatched and the village thatcher earlier this century, was Fred Gibbard, who is referred to

LOWER WAY, PADBURY.

PADBURY

in the writings of Alison Uttley. Mr. Gibbard was seldom seen not wearing his bowler-hat and it is a family joke that he wore it even when he went to bed. Many of the cottages have now been extended to make quite large & expensive properties — precise & manicured in ways which could not have been envisaged when they were first built.

PADBURY

There are people, whose families have lived for generations in Buckingham or its villages, who can be heard to say 'nowadays you never know who is living here', meaning that tucked-away in quiet corners of the countryside, sometimes there are 'new-comers' whose fame in one walk of life or another, extends far beyond Buckinghamshire and far beyond the shores of Britain In a quiet leafy backwater of Padbury there is a man of extraordinary genius, whose patented electronic systems are, to me, so bewilderingly complex, I cannot describe them. He is Don King, who in 1979 won an Inventor of the Year Award. It might be thought a cliché to refer to the 'struggling inventor', but, whilst Don is now successful, he has certainly had difficulties, not least because of the ineptness of Britain's investment and banking institutions. His micro chips may look no more than bits of Yorky Bar but the major car corporations of Europe, Japan and the United States, certainly know of G.A. King and have heard of Padbury, England.

DON KING OF PADBURY.

GAWCOTT PARISH CHURCH

Not far from Padbury is the village of Gawcott where the parish church of The Holy Trinity, or the circumstances of its construction, may have brought about the start of another career of national significance.

GREAT SCOTT

Gilbert Scott was born at the parsonage at Gawcott in 1811. His father was appointed curate there at a time when Gawcott Church was in ruins. With help from his parishoners the Rev Scott designed and built a new one — the church we see today which, inside, is as plain & square as a Wesleyan chapel. As an adolescent the young Gilbert may not have been too impressed by his father's architectural efforts, and it is said he would often walk the mile or so across the fields to admire the Church of All Saints at Hillesden, built in 1493 and known with good reason as THE CATHEDRAL IN THE FIELDS.

ALL SAINTS, HILLESDEN

It was a contrast to Gawcott Church: All Saints at Hillesden had a wealth of features and detail for an aspiring young architect to study in the nineteenth century. Sir Gilbert Scott is best known now for St Pancras Station and for the Albert Memorial, Kensington, but he was responsible for much more. He supervised the restoration of 29 cathedrals & nearly 500 churches, and was thought by some to have been far too thorough — at the same time careless of the antiquity which was being lost. The Society for the Protection of Ancient Buildings was formed largely with Sir Gilbert's activities in mind. One of his first commissions was a local workhouse for 125 paupers at Buckingham. He also designed the rounded front (the superintendent's lodgings) on the Old Gaol at Buckingham, and he was responsible for the gothic buttressing of the Church of St Peter & St Paul when it was showing serious cracks in the 1860s.

Hillesden Church was also the scene of fury and much distress during the Civil War. Sir Alexander Denton was declared to be a 'Royal Malignant', so his home — Hillesden House — was burned to the ground; most of the household took refuge in the Church, but Cromwell's men pursued them there and laid siege. The men & boys were captured & imprisoned; the women & children took refuge — some at Claydon House, others at Radclive Manor, which was also owned by the Dentons. Bullet holes can still be seen around the Church at Hillesden, and the present pulpit is said to be made from the door which took a battering at the time of the siege.

The little church of St Giles at Water Stratford also has a 'past'. In 1691, the rector John Mason declared that the Second Coming was nigh; he added that Water Stratford had been chosen as the New Jerusalem. He was a preacher of some persuasion for he convinced more than just his own parishioners. At the height of his following his flock numbered 400; they were there summer & winter, camping out in every available building in the village. Not long before he died he confided to his followers that he would rise on the third day after his death and would ascend into Heaven. Afterwards there were some who said they had seen & spoken with him on land behind the Rectory. His followers did not disperse for

THE DOORWAY OF ST GILES' CHURCH, WATER STRATFORD.

ST GILES' CHURCH, WATER STRATFORD

some time after his death, and it is said that a few of his staunchest followers were still camping in the village 16 years later. In the nineteenth century the Church of St Giles suffered at the hands of an over-enthusiastic restorer, and in more recent years the village of Water Stratford again became associated with 'visions' (but this time definitely of an illusive type), when Paul Daniels the magician lived there in the '80s.

Down the hill from Water Stratford, on the road from Oxford & the Cotswolds, lies the village of Tingewick – its people still keenly waiting for the day it receives its

THE SUNDAY SCHOOL, TINGEWICK.

THE CHURCH OF ST MARY MAGDALENE, TINGEWICK.

promised by-pass. The village has suffered from heavy traffic for a decade or so but not for the first time; on a summer's day in 1644, 12,000 Royalists, including 3000 horse, marched through the village on their way to Buckingham. Now, the properties along the main road suffer day and night from vibration, fumes, noise and dust, but even so the village store there, in 1986 was voted one of Britain's best.

One of Tingewick's best known residents is the Hon Elizabeth Keyes who has campaigned for many years against the water authority's putting fluoride in the public water supply; also against pollution through fertilizers and by fall-out from industrial chimneys. Miss Keyes' father was Admiral Lord Roger Keyes who, in the 1st World War, led the successful raids on Zeebrugge & Ostend harbours – imprisoning the German submarines stationed in the Bruges Canal. The action greatly hampered the Germans, and contributed to the lessening of the submarine menace. His son Lt. Col. Geoffrey Keyes lost his life in 1942 while leading a Commando raid on Gen. Rommel's HQ in Libya. He was awarded the Victoria Cross posthumously. A road in Buckingham bears the name Keyes.

TINGEWICK

Early one winter's morning I saw a vixen standing in the centre of a quiet lane near Tingewick; she continued to stare at my approaching car and made no attempt to jump aside as I got close. She brought me to a stop just a foot or two away from her, and then strolled around the car to the side door. There she stopped, and looked at me for a few moments, then walked with some difficulty through a gap in the hedge. I am told she was probably suffering from arthritis and therefore no longer capable of catching her own food. She was asking to be fed – or released from her misery in some other way.

The villages on this side of Buckingham are still quite rural – this cottage in Mixbury was once the gardener's lodge and some of the outbuildings to a large house. It is now known as the Old Rectory Cottage, and it has the feel of provincial France when you step into the garden.

THE OLD RECTORY COTTAGE, MIXBURY

This is Adstock, a village free from heavy through-traffic. Below is Adstock Cottage. New thatch looks too precise for my liking; I particularly enjoyed drawing this one because it is at its best — just a little scruffy. I would like it never to change.

ADSTOCK COTTAGE

THE AIRFIELDS

The map of north Buckinghamshire is dotted with wartime airfields; a few of their old control towers still stand and parts of some airfields are used by private flying clubs, but in the main their concrete runways are crumbling under the wheels of farm machinery. HORWOOD airfield is farmland once again; in the 2nd World War it might easily have been used for Special Operations due to its proximity to Bletchley Park. WHITFIELD, apart from a few batteries of hen houses, looks over-grown but largely intact – a good candidate as the setting for Frederick Forsyth's book The Shepherd. HINTON in the HEDGES, and FINMERE are both used by small private aircraft and Finmere is now well known for its Wendy Fair – a pioneer in Sunday Markets. Some of the old aircraft hangers at Finmere are used to hold part of the EEC intervention stock of wheat and barley – the Grain Mountain.

WHITFIELD AERODROME

The name of SILVERSTONE is now best known across the World as the home of British car racing – its 700 acres are owned by the British Racing Drivers' Club, and operated by its commercial limb, the Silverstone Circuits Ltd.. The gates I have drawn here lead to the Drivers' Clubhouse and the Guild of Motoring Writers' suite; they were once the paddock gates of the old Goodwood Circuit. In recent years the British Grand Prix has been held alternately at Brands Hatch and Silverstone, but now it is to be held at Silverstone each year, at least until 1992. One of the most sought after awards in the field of motor racing is the BRDC Gold Star. Just inside the main doors to the Drivers' Clubhouse is a list of its winners; it would provide a good basis for anyone writing a history of car racing. The first winners were Sir Malcolm Campbell,

SILVERSTONE: THE CIRCUIT WAS ORIGINALLY INTENDED FOR HORWOOD AIRFIELD, BUT LOCAL OPPOSITION PREVENTED IT.

Sir Henry Seagrave, and S.C.H. Davis. Champion Star winner in the Club's history is Stirling Moss, who won the BRDC Gold Star 10 times between the years 1950 and 1961. Since then there have been the names of World Champions: Jack Brabham, John Surtees, Jackie Stewart, James Hunt, Emerson Fittipaldi, Niki Lauda . .

Vintage car club rallies are also held at Silverstone and, from time to time, the road leading into Buckingham from Winslow is filled with the distinctive gurgle of antique vehicles: cars such as the Duck's-Back Alvis, an 'S' Type Invicta, a Prince Henry Vauxhall, a Speed Six Bentley, a Lancia Lambda, a Frazer-Nash – sometimes a line of early Rolls Royces. Once I saw a queue of four Bugattis waiting at Cannon Corner.

The Winslow Wheel is not another car club but it is a potter's wheel designed in 1961 by

WINSLOW

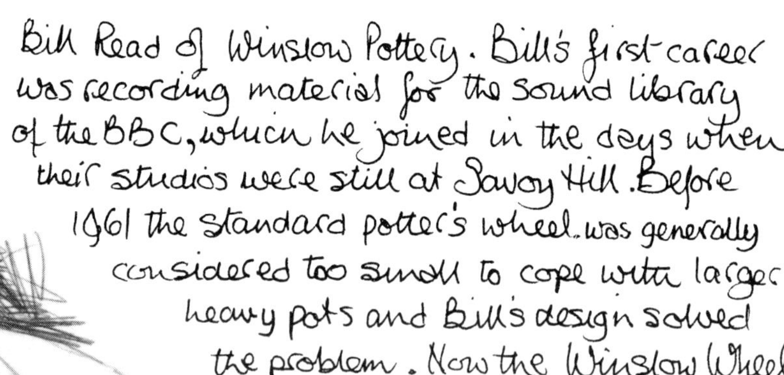

BILL READ

Bill Read of Winslow Pottery. Bill's first career was recording materials for the sound library of the BBC, which he joined in the days when their studios were still at Savoy Hill. Before 1961 the standard potter's wheel was generally considered too small to cope with larger heavy pots and Bill's design solved the problem. Now the Winslow Wheel is used throughout Britain and it is also selling successfully abroad.

To the people of Buckingham, Winslow is more than just another town on the A413, it is an old friend. It is like a stalwart, stationed on the edge of high ground, posted as a lookout to check the passage of those using the road across the Vale, from Buckingham's old adversary — the usurper, Aylesbury. A little further south from Winslow it is possible to see the outline of the County Town, the spire of the Parish Church and, towering above it, the County offices – an eleven storey concrete blockhouse – as alien from its surroundings as a Berlin bunker might be if it were placed in Bourton on the Water. Perhaps now, 'Fred's Folly' as it is known, should be considered in the same way as the City of London regard the '60s buildings in Paternoster Square.

However, it must be said that, if Buckingham were still the county town, it would be as dusty and noisy as Aylesbury with its assize courts, lawyers offices, a sprawling gaol, and all the trappings of local government. As it is, Buckingham, like Winslow, is still a country town and so we should be thankful.

On days in early summer the hedgerows have willow herb and eyebright, meadow vetchling & toadflax, there is groundsel everywhere and pineappleweed. In winter, sometimes the sounds of the Whaddon Chase can be heard. On the death of its last Master, Dorian Williams, the well known BBC commentator, the Whaddon joined with the Bicester — but their Boxing Day meet is still a local event; Winslow Market Square, soon after breakfast on Boxing Day morning, is a favourite rendezvous for many people, not just the hunt followers.

Just off the square in Winslow is the Bell Hotel where, it is said, a special suite was maintained in the 1930s for unscheduled stops by Edward, Prince of Wales. After the war it became known as a pub for men only. The story goes that one day a charabanc stopped in Winslow and the landlord was so upset by the motley crowd which entered the Bell, that he locked the front doors after they left, and did not open them again: his regulars knew their way through the court yard. The Bell did not have a bar in the regular sense; the drinks were served from the side-board. In the '60s and '70s some 'liberated' ladies would see the Bell as a challenge. I recall how a French woman made a special trip to try her luck; the regulars stood in silence until she left.

WINSLOW PARISH CHURCH

A PUB CRAWL

THE WHEATSHEAF INN, MAIDS MORETON

It seems that England's eccentric laws on drinking-times have always been given the respect they deserve. Tales abound, many dating from well before the experience of most of us, of village publicans receiving covert notice of an imminent check-up by the County Constabulary. Each pub seems to have its own version of the same story: after receipt of such a warning, a string of chuckling villagers, filled-mugs in hand, would remove itself to some adjacent premises. After a short time a loud knock would be heard at the pub door. On entering, the senior officer, finding nothing amiss, would dismiss his men and go home to bed. A short while later, the local bobbies would return through the back door; a signal would be given and within a few moments the exiled revellers would join them for another drink. Conspiracies such as these, I gather, produced friendly & respectful attitudes between all concerned and with few exceptions I am told, most pubs were quite orderly places.

THE CROWN INN, GAWCOTT

Only occasionally would the harmony be broken when perhaps someone's wife, aggrieved by her husband's frequent absence from home, or by his increasing girth, would make a formal complaint about his 'local'. The lightning raid which followed would catch everyone unawares. There was one such occasion when a damp & muddy gun-club

THE ROBIN HOOD, PADBURY

THE TWO BREWERS, THORNBOROUGH

sat with their dogs around a log fire in the public bar drinking lemon squash well into the afternoon. The loud knock surprised everyone but only two attempted to escape; one, an agile youth disappeared successfully through the kitchen window, and the other, a portly farmer, went into the ladies' loo, saying that on no account should he be found. While we talked and had our names taken, no one gave him a second thought. Afterwards, we discussed the raid and the landlord kindly made us cups of coffee; it was quite a while before someone remembered his unusual exit. Where had he gone? He had locked the door behind him and tried to clamber through a small high window. He was stuck half-way through – legs and backside on the inside, arms and a very red face in the yard; not knowing when the coast was clear he had been unwilling to call for help.

THE OLD THATCHED INN, ADSTOCK.

Also, it is not unknown for the marriages of landlords to come under strain. There is one frequently re-told story of the wife of a village publican who, wishing to emphasise her feelings of discontent, disrobed and, carrying a suitcase of her belongings, strode naked through the crowded bar to a waiting vehicle. It is said that the incident stopped conversation for a moment, but not the drinking.

I have been advised to say that

THE FOLLY INN, ADSTOCK

THE SEVEN STARS, TWYFORD

none of these events took place in the pubs I have drawn here, and probably did not take place at all — that is the nature of any gossip, but pub gossip in the villages is sometimes not only creative; it may be a carefully researched extension of a truth .... There is a tale of a recluse who lived in an isolated cottage in woodland near the Town. He had been there since 1943 — an educated man who, for 39 years, avoided showing his face to any outsider. He died in 1982, at which time there was a thorough search of his cottage and garden for 'documents'; for it became known that he was one of Britain's old fascists, and a friend of Unity Mitford. All this is known to be true, but the story which went around soon after his death was that in 1935 he was amongst the friends of Unity who frequented the Osteria Bavaria and a flat in Wasserburgerstrasse, Bogenhausen. He befriended Gretl Braun, who was living there with her sister Eva. The story takes one more easy step: their liaison was 'sealed' in secret. Conclusion: our hermit was 'brother-in-law' to Hitler.

This book of drawings and gossip is almost at an end; on page 6 you will find my apologies for some of its shortcomings.

THE SHOULDER OF MUTTON, LITTLE HORWOOD

To an outsider, this book may have given the wrong impression that Buckingham and its villages are composed wholly of attractive views and buildings. I have chosen only some of the best and, deliberately, I have missed out the inelegant: too often our senses are assaulted by their reality. (The spray-can scribblings of adolescents are not a fraction so obtrusive as official street graffiti — yellow lines, zebra crossings, traffic signs & instructions.). However, Buckingham does not support itself on its rustic charm. The Town has always needed industrial buildings — it is, after all, a working town. For in between those rare and joyous moments in the past when the Town received aristocratic patronage, Buckingham has needed to earn its own living.

For centuries the main income was from sheep and wool; later, there was leather tanning. The manufacture of steam cars was not a great success. In the middle of this century a few medium-sized employers moved to the Town — a factory for dairy products (but with the loss of the railway it moved away again), Sigma and Cementone-Beaver with their paints and coatings, Hartridge with their diesel testing instruments and Wipac with their automotive products. A more recent industry has been the marshalling of antiques for export. But even with these injections of new blood, the 1960s saw Buckingham in the doldrums: it was evident that the old Town lacked vitality and self-confidence — it had insufficient grip on its own boot-strings — — it had no leaders with the means to beget new initiatives. Buckingham needed help, from without.

Following a meeting at Eaton House, London, between a group of economists and leading academics, a special presentation was made to members of the Buckingham Borough Council in 1971. It is said they had little no prior knowledge of its purpose; they were shown plans, together with sketches, a timetable and cash-flow charts. It was a memorable occasion, for the proposal was that Buckingham should become a university town. At the time, The Advertiser reported: 'To say that the Council Members were stunned, is an understatement —

— they were knocked speechless....'

THE RADCLIFFE CENTRE, BUCKINGHAM UNIVERSITY

In 1970, the Town had more than its share of redundant and delapidated buildings: the Congregational (later the United Reform) Church was attracting not a fraction of the 600 voices for which it was designed; the Old Town Mill was silent save for the Ouse pouring through a rusting sluice; the sounds of the old Royal Bucks Hussars with their horses (commanded by the Duke and consisting of 540 officers and men) had long since left their stables off Hunter Street; the Roman Catholic College built beside the London Road in 1894, no longer echoed the feet of boys intending to join the Franciscan Order. There were many more unwanted buildings, and work began on them, for the University, in 1972. Much has happened since; the old stables have become the Denning Law Library, and the old dairies in Hunter Street are now the Life Sciences Building; the Franciscan College has a variety of uses and the Old Town Mill is now a refectory and common rooms. And there are many new buildings erected on the Hunter Street Campus, and around the Franciscan Building. Buckingham people sometimes are breathless at the ease with which the University obtains permission to alter familiar landscapes.

The University of Buckingham is Britain's only university independent

THE OLD TOWN MILL

PREBEND COTTAGE & THE LIFE SCIENCE LABORATORY BUCKINGHAM UNIVERSITY

of direct government finance. Its first students were admitted in 1976 and the College received full university status when it was granted its Royal Charter in 1983. Paul Drayton was commissioned to write a choral and orchestral work to mark the occasion. The founding principal of the College had been Lord Beloff; the University's first Vice-Chancellor was Professor Alan Peacock. Buckingham University's Chancellor, is Lord Hailsham.

CHURCH STREET: ROUTE OF THE ACADEMIC PROCESSION ON GRADUATION DAY.

The founding of a university in (and its effects upon) a small south Midlands country town might make a very good basis for a novel. Certainly Buckingham and its people will never be the same again. In 1864 the population of the Town was 3849, by 1929 it was 3060. By 1961 it was still no more than 4400 and the local accent still dominated: shop-boys would scurry when overbearing village personages yelled their shopping needs from LandRovers hitched to horse boxes parked in the centre of the square. Seldom did the Town see 'foreigners'.

The Townspeople have altered – but not all of them overnight (some people are always slow to change, in the early '80s flared trousers and mini-skirts were still worn in Buckingham - not as conscious acts of revival, but as steadfast loyalty to the fashions of the '60s). Now much of Buckingham seems resigned, even keen, to

PROF. SIR ALAN PEACOCK

CLIVE BIRCH

become more like the outside world. Many of the University's 600 students are from abroad: some are hard-up like students anywhere, but conspicuously others are quite well-off. Locals would no longer be surprised to see a 6 foot 3 African princess driving a Maserati from the Students Union, or a chauffeur-driven Rolls Royce Silver Cloud waiting for an Arab undergraduate outside a lecture hall. The remnants of the old village gentry have become almost unassuming, and the shop assistants are now far from being obsequious. The new confidence has spread around the Town: large housing estates have sprung-up and the population is now (1988) about 10,000. The local Bucks accent is still to be heard, but more often you hear the glottal stop 'T' of Greater London. The revival has attracted other dynamic enterprises to the Town: Barracuda Books arrived in 1978. Now with 250 titles under its belt (150 still in print) it has become the Country's leading publisher of local history. Clive Birch, the publisher, is known for driving a hard bargain and when I showed my drawing of him to a business acquaintance he said "yes, that's him, and when he smiles like that you know you've lost".

The International Management Centre from Buckingham, has also grown successful since it arrived in the Town: its management studies programmes are running in many countries around the world. Like the University, IMCB has renovated several of Buckingham's old buildings: Marriotts, Hill House, and Swinfen Harris's old coach house on Castle Hill.

MARRIOTTS, CASTLE STREET.

LORD HAILSHAM

Friendship between Town & Gown is not being taken for granted; it is being worked upon. Old attitudes, in some quarters die hard. There is a story of an unexpected meeting between a group of villagers from the west of Buckingham, and Lord Hailsham, Chancellor of the University. The group were constituents of the late Neil Martin MP, and he had invited them to meet him at the Palace of Westminster. As he led them along a corridor, Lord Hailsham, impressively attired in the robes of Lord Chancellor, came out of a doorway behind them: needing to speak to Mr. Martin, the Lord Chancellor called out his name "Neil!" It is said that, at this point, a number of the constituents got upon their knees.

NIGEL BOWERMAN WHO HAS CAREFULLY SWEPT THE STREETS OF BUCKINGHAM SINCE 1978, SOON AFTER HE LEFT SCHOOL.

Subscribers

Presentation Copies

1 BUCKINGHAM TOWN COUNCIL
2 AYLESBURY VALE DISTRICT COUNCIL
3 BUCKINGHAMSHIRE COUNTY COUNCIL
4 BUCKINGHAMSHIRE COUNTY LIBRARY, BUCKINGHAM BRANCH
5 BUCKINGHAMSHIRE COUNTY LIBRARY, WINSLOW LIBRARY
6 BUCKINGHAM HERITAGE TRUST

7 Alan Percy Walker
8 Clive & Carolyn Birch
9 Don & Hilary King
10 Sue Halliday & Duncan Christelow
11 Dr & Mrs P.R. Lewis
12 F.J. Imrie
13 John & Audrey Cornwall
14, 15 J.M. Briggs
16 Mrs M. Harrison
17 L.A. Brock
18 Mrs M.A. Wood
19 Miss W.M. Hudson
20 Mr J.C. Gardiner
21 Mr D.W. Webb.
22 Mrs J. Anscomb
23 Mrs A. Garman
24 Mrs A. Jerrams
25 Mr A.M. Marlow
26 Mrs J. Burgess
27 Mr & Mrs D. Jackson
28 Mrs A.C. Barrett
29 Mrs D.M. Dyson
30 Mr J. Raffell
31 Mrs B. Maddison
32 Mrs P.E. Boyle
33 Miss H.E. Walker
34 Mr Norman Saving
35 Mrs Thompson
36 Mrs D. Comerford
37 Mr S.A. Mawby
38 Jeffrey & Gillian Geary
39 Dr & Mrs P.R. Wiles
40 Michael Moyles
41 Elizabeth Dady
42 Geoffrey M. Hartley
43 Simon G. Hartley
44 Barbara M. Hartley
45 Franz Dunshirn
46 Michael A. Carter
47 Dr Elizabeth Dickson
48 Town & Country Cars
49 John F. Roper
50 Fiona Lissauer
51 Mr H. Elim
52 Mr A. Forman
53 Nicolas Owen
53 Mary Miller
55 Leoni Seymour
56, 57 Avril Buckroyd
58 Kathy Hack
59 David King
60 R.J. Hatton
61 Mrs E.M. Hosie
62 Cynthia Waterman
63 Aubrey Whitehead
64 Michael Manisty
65 Joan E. Savage
66 Scott Stanbridge
67 J.W. Tibbetts
68 D.R. Buckley
69 N.R.L. Cawley
70 Hilary Tomlinson
71 Matthew Lewis
72 Mrs Stephanie Richardson
73 Mrs Sheila Smith
74 Edward Phillips
75 Mrs Chris Howell
76, 77 Victor Tattersall
78 Dorothy V. Bowerman
79 Mrs S.D.A. Howarth
80 Mavis Rock
81 R. May
82 Mrs A.E. Watts
83 Mrs Jackie Lowing
84, 85 D.H. McKay
86 Mrs Glenna Favell
87 David Wise
88, 89 Mrs A. Barr
90 Ellison Platt
91 Mrs Y. Penne-Stuart
92, 93 Walter Southwell Brown
94 Robert Warner
95 Dr Collin Place
96 Joan Wagland
97 Mrs Monica Jones
98, 99 Mrs M. Fox
100 John & Celia Clarke
101 S. Callis
102 David & Angela Brock
103 F.W. Weidmann
104 Sonia Csom
105 Evelyn & Peter Steers
106 Mrs N.D. Penn
107 Terry Davey
108 Edward Stamp
109 Mr F.X. Kay
110 Dr C.W. Weidmann
111 Richard Cowell
112 Simon Smith
113 Graham & Dorothy Shaw
114 Mrs L.M. Moyles
115 Duncan Law
116 Mr D.J. Connolly
117 Betty & Arthur Hutchings
118 Bill Read
119 L.S. & J.P. Everett
120 Mr. W.E. Rothe
121 Mike Quinn; Tingewick P.O.
122 Des Hutchings
123 Krystyna Gibson
124 Clare Gibson
125 Louisa Cielbala
126 Jan & Abbie Cielbala
127 Michael Games
128 Bert Clarke
129 Keith Driscoll
130 D.G. Dowsing
131, 132 Caroline E. Jackman
133 Dr Gordon Wills
134 Mrs Sandra Pass
135 Dr James Espey
136 Mr Frank Gerhard
137 Mr & Mrs Reg Turner
138 Peter A. Ponsson
139 John & Lynne Tipping
140 Mrs Patricia H. Busby
141 A.M. Jeffs
142 Barbara Hooper
143 Susan Clamp
144 Mrs C.J. McInnes
145 Mrs B. North
146 Mrs J.T. Chei
147 Mr & Mrs. Rob Saunders
148–150 Roderick John Tribe
151 Mrs T. Johnson
152 Michael Etherington
153 Ken Cockerton
154 Fiona Walker
155 Guy Walker
156 Saskia Andrews
157 Alexander Hosie-Walker
158 Richard Webb
159 Gail McDaniel
160 Maurice Acton
161 K.R. Heather
162 Freda Mary Sturch
163 Mary Saunders
164 John Robertson
165 Roger Moyse
166 Patti M.W. Pearce
167 T.J. Pallett
168 Moira Williams
169 Ian Thompson
170, 171 Hilary Walker
172 Mrs June Holbrooke
173 Patricia Zaman
174, 175 John Faulkner & Co, Estate Agents
176 Mrs B. Baughan
177 John Tearle
178 Ben Nagroo
179 Dennis H. Brown
180 Chris & Valerie Pendleton
181 Mrs Joan Barlow
182 Peter Russell
183, 184 Irene Simpson
185 Terence Smith
186, 187 Peter & Kay Bradley
188 Mrs P.J.W. Thomas
189 Desmond Bonner
190 Miss W.M. Baron
191 Dr D.S. Jackson
192 Dr H.R. Thomas
193 Mr D.S. Lewis
194 Mrs Monica Thorn
195 Mr Brian Taylor
196 Mrs B. Farmer
197 Mrs P. Crawford
198 Chris & Sue Fogden
199 Mrs M. Williams
200 A.J. Mole
201 Diana Pettifer
202 Mr Paul Collins
203 Stephen Thomas
204 Leslie Sarton
205 V.A. & C.A. Knibbs
206 T.R. Allitt
207 L. Smith
208 The Royal Latin School Library
209 Page Hill Middle School, Buckingham
210 Sheila Price
211 Mrs B. Waine
212 Terence & Elaine Barnett
213 M.H. Keir
214 Mark & Julie Palmer
215 George F. Thomas
216, 217 J.E.M. Watkins
218 Graham Bushell
219, 220 S.M. Gwyneth Corbett
221 Frederic Moraillon
222 Mrs S.S.P. Henshaw
223 Miss Jenny Hough
224 K. Liversedge
225 Veronica Lynch
226 J.K.L. Bidgood
227 Mr & Mrs J.A. Tutin
228 Tom Jarrett
229 Buckingham Golf Club
230 Mrs Molly Wilby
231 Derek Boughton
232 Mrs P. Brook
233 Mrs Veronica Gibbard
234 Roger Andrews
235 David J. Payne
236 Miss Karen Cooper
237 Alan Haynes
238 Richard Cox
239 Rod Hooper
240 Mr & Mrs A. Wedley
241 Bertrand T. Whitehead
242 A.C. Mayston
243 R.S. Taylor
244 Edward John Cockerill
245 Derrick Bales
246 David & Pauline Stevens
247 Angela Robinson
248 Richard Knowles
249 John & Judy Sharp
250 David Brookling
251 Brian Howlett
252 Jane Edwards
253 Nancy Gulak
254 Gill Cridland
255 Mary & Theodore Connor
256 Judith Harries
257 D.J. Collett
258 E. Clements
259 Mrs Dorothy Aris
260 D.W. Hayden
261 Mrs J. Teague
262 Anthony Bush
263 Douglas Ralph
264 Steven James
265 Miss D. Evans
266 John Evans
267 Mrs W.G. Walker
268 Flora Carter
269 Eric Betteridge
270 Mrs M. Watts
271 Mr & Mrs J.M. Little
272 Clark Galleries
273 Mrs Joan Fincher
274–276 Rob & Jacqui North
277, 278 Estill Putney
279 Mrs Jacqueline Lowing
280 J.M. Davies
281 Nicholas Shipp
282 Gerry Newman
283 Mrs E.M. Hadlow
284 Lt J.P.F. Hadlow RN
285 Eric Markham
286 Mrs J. Jerrams
287 A.G. Webster
288 Mr & Mrs T.A. James
289 P. Evans
290 W.R. Drake
291 Cecil Parry
292 Doreen Herron
293 J.A. Ratford
294 Mr F.V. Pollard
295 Mrs P.E. Austin
296 John Metcalfe
297 Mr R.T. Montgomery
298 Roy S. Walker
299 Brian & Stephanie Wall
300 J.M. Lewis
301–310 David Williams, Estate Agents
311 M.W. Swinhoe-Phelan
312 Stephen James Richardson
313 F.A.W. Smith
314 P. Gomersall
315 Barbara Brown
316 H.S. & D.W. Wood
317 N. Humphrey
318–339 Northamptonshire Libraries
340–359 Buckinghamshire County Library
360 J.A. Southall
361–381 Buckinghamshire County Library
382 T. Tarbox
383 S.A. Matthews
384 Librarie au Point, Quebec
385 Mrs S.A. Coles
386 D. Burch
387 Richard Stallworthy
388–390 Mrs P.A. Capps

Remaining names unlisted

Delicious Disney

Holidays

HAPPY
HOLIDAYS

Delicious Disney
Holidays

THE DISNEY CHEFS

WITH PAM BRANDON

PHOTOGRAPHY BY GARY BOGDON

INTRODUCTION

What better place to celebrate any holiday than the Disney Theme Parks and Resorts, or on a *Disney Cruise Line* getaway? But if you find yourself at home for the holidays, this compact collection of recipes will take you through the year—from hot cross buns for Easter to garlic-orange pork ribs for the Fourth of July, to smoked-salmon-and-herb muffins for a Hanukkah buffet. And because any holiday is an excuse for a memory-making culinary creation, we include offbeat ideas, too, like tofu in broth for Earth Day and Jack Skellington sugar cookies for Halloween.

Vacations, like holidays, often are defined by food, so maybe you fondly remember the sweet potato pancakes with honey-pecan butter at The Wave at Disney's Contemporary Resort that we like for a Mother's Day brunch, or the Rancho del Zocalo veggie tamales from *Disneyland* Park that we suggest as a Christmas treat. These dishes are on the menu year-round, but some special dishes are on menus for just a few short months, such as the holiday Yule Log from the bakery at Disney's Yacht & Beach Club Resorts or the *Disney Cruise Line* pumpkin-ginger soup. Regardless, you can now bring them to your table anytime.

So, whether you are creating a new holiday tradition for your family or reliving a favorite Disney vacation memory, get in the kitchen and have fun. We've included wine and beverage pairings with these special-occasion recipes to make it easy to start planning your own delicious feasts.

It doesn't always have to be a holiday to celebrate around the table!

—Pam Brandon

AROL
BOMA

TABLE OF CONTENTS

NEW YEAR'S EVE

BLT Flatbread

VILLAGE HAUS RESTAURANT ❄ *DISNEYLAND* PARK ❄ *DISNEYLAND* RESORT

GARLIC AIOLI

1 small head fresh garlic

¼ teaspoon olive oil

½ cup mayonnaise

1 tablespoon Dijon mustard

Coarse salt, to taste

CARAMELIZED ONIONS

1 large onion, thinly sliced

2 tablespoons olive oil

Coarse salt, freshly ground black pepper, to taste

MARINATED TOMATOES

2 medium tomatoes

¼ cup thinly sliced fresh basil

2 teaspoons extra-virgin olive oil

1 teaspoon freshly minced garlic

Coarse salt, freshly ground black pepper, to taste

This savory flatbread is perfect for a New Year's Eve party menu. Make components ahead of time, then pop in the oven for an easy nosh topped with fresh greens.

MAKES 1 (12-INCH) FLATBREAD

For garlic aioli:

1. Preheat oven to 425°F. Cut top off head of garlic to expose the cloves; drizzle with olive oil and wrap in foil. Roast in preheated oven for an hour, or until garlic is golden brown and very soft. Squeeze garlic out of skins and mash with a fork.

2. Whisk together 2 tablespoons of roasted garlic, mayonnaise, and mustard. Season with salt. Can be made a day ahead and refrigerated.

For caramelized onions:

1. Combine onions and oil in a large sauté pan. Season with salt and pepper.

2. Cook, stirring often over very low heat, until onions are golden brown and very soft, about 30 minutes. Can be made a day ahead and refrigerated.

For marinated tomatoes:

1. Cut tomatoes in half and gently squeeze to remove seeds.

2. Dice into ½-inch cubes and stir together in a medium bowl with basil, oil, and garlic. Season with salt and pepper. Can be made a day ahead and refrigerated.

(continued on page 10)

FENNEL-ARUGULA SALAD

1 (1-pound) fennel bulb

1 cup fresh arugula

1 cup chopped frisée lettuce

2 teaspoons extra-virgin olive oil

Coarse salt, freshly ground black pepper, to taste

12-inch prepared flatbread

1 cup chopped cooked bacon

½ cup shredded mozzarella cheese

½ cup shredded provolone cheese

For fennel-arugula salad:

1. Cut the top stalks and root end off of fennel and discard. Cut fennel in half lengthwise and thinly slice.
2. Coarsely chop arugula and combine with frisée in a large bowl. Toss lettuces with fennel, olive oil, salt, and pepper.

For BLT flatbreads:

1. Preheat oven to 450°F.
2. Place flatbread crust on a baking sheet. Spread with garlic aioli, leaving a ½-inch border around edges. Top with bacon, mozzarella, provolone, caramelized onions, and finish with marinated tomatoes.
3. Bake 6 to 8 minutes, or until edges are golden brown and cheese is melted. Remove from oven and top with salad. Serve immediately.

WHAT TO DRINK: Mix a festive Remy champagne cocktail by combining champagne and pear vodka.

Chai Cream

SANAA ❄ DISNEY'S ANIMAL KINGDOM LODGE ❄ WALT DISNEY WORLD RESORT

Splurge and celebrate New Year's Eve with a creamy, dreamy dessert accented by the subtle flavors of chai, cinnamon, cardamom, and peppercorns.

SERVES 8

5 ⅓ cups, plus ½ cup heavy cream, divided

1 vanilla bean, split lengthwise and scraped, seeds reserved

1 cup granulated sugar

1 (1-ounce) envelope powdered gelatin

2 teaspoons black chai tea, ground in a coffee or spice grinder

1 cinnamon stick

6 green cardamom pods

6 whole black peppercorns

1 tablespoon powdered sugar

1 tablespoon semisweet chocolate shavings

1. Combine 5 cups of cream, vanilla bean seeds, and granulated sugar in a medium saucepan over medium-high heat. Bring to a simmer, stirring occasionally.
2. Place ⅓ cup of cream in a small bowl and add powdered gelatin; stir to mix.
3. When cream-sugar mixture simmers, immediately remove from heat, and add cream-gelatin mixture, stirring well until gelatin is completely dissolved. Add tea, cinnamon, cardamom pods, and peppercorns.
4. Let mixture steep for 10 minutes, stirring occasionally. Pour mixture into a metal bowl set in a larger bowl of ice water. Cover with plastic wrap, and let steep and cool for 30 minutes.
5. Pour mixture through a fine-mesh sieve into a clean bowl. Freeze for 20 minutes, or until the mixture starts to thicken. (This allows the gelatin to set slightly so the specks of tea remain in suspension instead of falling to the bottom of the glasses.)
6. Divide mixture evenly among 8 (5-ounce) glasses or ramekins, and refrigerate for at least 4 hours before serving.
7. To serve, combine remaining ½ cup cream and powdered sugar in a large bowl. Whip with an electric mixer until stiff peaks form. Dollop whipped cream onto each glass, then sprinkle with semisweet chocolate shavings. (Use a cheese grater or vegetable peeler to shave from a solid bar of semisweet chocolate.)

Scharffen Berger Chocolate Truffle Cake

NAPA ROSE ❊ DISNEY'S GRAND CALIFORNIAN HOTEL & SPA ❊ DISNEYLAND RESORT

½ cup, plus 6 tablespoons unsalted butter, softened (extra for ramekins)

6 ½ ounces Scharffen Berger bittersweet chocolate, chopped fine

5 large eggs, room temperature, separated

½ cup sugar, divided (extra for ramekins)

1 tablespoon all-purpose flour, sifted

Chocolate is a traditional treat given to win hearts on Valentine's Day, and nothing could be more luxurious than a Scharffen Berger chocolate truffle cake. If you can't find Scharffen Berger chocolate, any high-quality bittersweet (at least 58 percent chocolate) will work. Delicious with vanilla or vanilla-cherry ice cream.

SERVES 8

1. Preheat oven to 375°F. Lightly butter bottom and sides of 8 individual 6-ounce ramekins. Coat thinly with sugar and shake out excess. Set aside.

2. Prepare a double boiler and bring water to a simmer over low heat. Place butter and chocolate in top of double boiler and gently stir until melted smoothly and combined.

3. Whisk egg yolks and ¼ cup sugar in a large mixing bowl for 3 to 4 minutes or until smooth and slightly thickened. Add flour and combine.

4. Ladle a small amount of melted chocolate into egg yolk mixture and whisk to combine. Add another ladle of chocolate into egg yolk mixture and continue to whisk. Once the temperature of the egg yolk mixture has been warmed, add remaining chocolate to egg yolks and whisk vigorously until completely combined. Set aside.

5. Warm egg whites in a small metal bowl (first make sure it is very clean and dry) that just fits into a small saucepan with hot water in it. Allow eggs to warm for 1 to 2 minutes. Remove and add 1 tablespoon sugar, whip mixture using a handheld mixer on medium speed until soft peaks form.

6. Slowly add an additional 1½ tablespoons sugar while continuing to whip egg whites. Increase speed to high and slowly add remaining 1½ tablespoons sugar. Whip egg whites and sugar for another 3 to 4 minutes or until stiff peaks form.

7. Gently fold in ¼ of chocolate mixture into egg whites to combine. Add remaining chocolate and continue to fold till completely combined, being careful not to overwork mixture.

8. Divide batter equally among the prepared ramekins, filling ¾ full. Place on a baking sheet and bake for 14 minutes, or until tops are puffy, but center is still soft. Do not overbake.

9. Cut around edges of cakes using a small knife to loosen cakes. Carefully invert cakes onto serving plates and serve immediately.

ST. PATRICK'S DAY

Irish Stew

DISNEY CRUISE LINE SERVICES

2 tablespoons vegetable oil, divided

3 pounds lamb chuck

2 onions, diced

3 cups low-sodium beef stock

2 carrots, peeled and diced

3 potatoes, diced

1 small head green cabbage, diced

2 leeks, finely diced

2 tablespoons fresh thyme, chopped

Coarse salt, freshly ground black pepper, to taste

This hearty stew with lamb is a celebrated classic for St. Patrick's Day.

SERVES 6

1. Heat 1 tablespoon vegetable oil in a large stockpot until oil shimmers. Add half of lamb meat, being careful not to crowd the pan; sear 3 to 4 minutes on each side. Transfer meat to a plate. Repeat with remaining vegetable oil and lamb.

2. Add onions to the pan; sauté about 2 minutes, or until translucent. Add stock and lamb meat and bring to a boil. Reduce heat to medium-low, and simmer 40 minutes, skimming any foam from surface.

3. Add carrots and potatoes and cook 20 minutes more. Add cabbage, leeks, and thyme; simmer 5 minutes. Season to taste with salt and pepper.

WHAT TO DRINK: With a malty aroma and a hint of vanilla, Guinness Draught beer works wonders with this stew.

Irish Whiskey Custard

ROSE & CROWN PUB & DINING ROOM ❇ UNITED KINGDOM PAVILION

Just 5 ingredients create a decadent, creamy treat with a flourish of Irish whiskey, fit for a St. Paddy's Day celebration.

SERVES 8

- 3 ⅓ cups heavy cream
- ½ cup half-and-half
- ⅞ cup, plus 8 tablespoons, sugar
- 8 egg yolks
- 3 tablespoons Irish whiskey

1. Preheat oven to 300°F. Combine all ingredients in a large bowl, except for 8 tablespoons of sugar. Whisk until combined.
2. Pour mixture through a fine mesh strainer into another large bowl. Divide mixture evenly among 8, 8-ounce custard bowls or ramekins.
3. Place 4 custard bowls into each of 2, 13x9x2-inch baking pans. Pour water into both pans until level reaches three quarters of the way up sides of custard bowls.
4. Bake for 45 to 50 minutes or until custard is set but not browned.
5. Remove custard bowls from water baths and cool in refrigerator at least 3 hours.
6. To serve, evenly sprinkle top of each custard with 1 tablespoon of remaining sugar. Use a kitchen torch to caramelize the sugar, keeping the flame about 2 inches above surface so sugar melts and browns. Allow sugar to cool and harden for 1 minute before serving.

EASTER

Carrot Cake with White-Chocolate Cheesecake "Icing"

DISNEY CRUISE LINE SERVICES

WHITE-CHOCOLATE CHEESECAKE TOPPING

2 eggs, room temperature

5 tablespoons sugar

1 ½ cups heavy cream, divided

1 tablespoon powdered gelatin

8-ounce package cream cheese, room temperature

1 lemon, zested and juiced

¼ cup finely chopped white chocolate

CARROT CAKE

2 cups sugar

1 ½ cups, plus 2 tablespoons, all-purpose flour

1 teaspoon baking powder

½ teaspoon baking soda

½ teaspoon ground cinnamon

Pinch of salt

5 eggs, lightly whisked

¾ cup canola oil

½ cup pineapple juice

½ teaspoon vanilla extract

2 cups shredded carrots

1 cup chopped walnuts

The warm colors of springtime make this dessert the ideal sweet for an Easter gathering.

MAKES 8 MINICAKES

For cheesecake topping:

1. Whisk together eggs and sugar in a medium bowl until thickened. Set aside.
2. Heat ¼ cup cream in a separate medium bowl and sprinkle with gelatin. Set aside for 3 minutes, then stir to melt gelatin.
3. Beat cream cheese until fluffy in a large bowl, then beat in lemon zest and lemon juice. Set aside.
4. Microwave ¼ cup cream in a medium microwave-safe bowl until hot; add chopped white chocolate and stir until melted. Set aside to cool slightly, then beat into cream cheese mixture until smooth.
5. Whip remaining cup of cream in a large bowl until soft peaks form. Set aside.
6. Fold beaten egg mixture into cream cheese mixture, then stir in gelatin until completely smooth. Gently fold in the whipped cream. Refrigerate for at least 4 hours.

For carrot cake:

1. Preheat oven to 350°F. Spray a 9x13x2-inch pan with nonstick baking spray with flour; set aside.

2. Combine sugar, flour, baking powder, baking soda, cinnamon, and salt in the bowl of an electric mixer fitted with the paddle attachment.

3. Whisk together eggs, oil, pineapple juice, and vanilla extract in a medium bowl; stir in carrots and walnuts. With mixer running, slowly pour egg mixture into flour mixture and mix until just combined. Pour batter into prepared pan.

4. Bake for about 20 minutes. Cool cake in pan. Once the cake is cooled, refrigerate.

5. To assemble, place the cheesecake mixture into piping bag fitted with a large round tip, or in a large zip-top bag. (Snip off corner of bag when ready to use.)

6. Cut carrot cake into rounds using a biscuit cutter or cookie cutter. Generously pipe cheesecake filling on top of carrot cake rounds, about 2 inches high on each cake.

Hot Cross Buns

BOARDWALK BAKERY ❄ WALT DISNEY WORLD RESORT

These slightly sweet buns are an English tradition associated with Good Friday, the Friday before Easter Sunday, and are marked with a symbolic cross. Hot cross buns can be eaten plain, or are delicious with fresh fruit or toasted with butter or jam.

MAKES 16 BUNS

DOUGH

1 cup warm milk

1 (2 ¼-ounce) packet instant yeast

3 ¾ cups bread flour

¼ cup sugar

½ teaspoon salt

2 teaspoons cinnamon

1 egg

1 ½ cups raisins

3 tablespoons softened butter

EGG WASH

1 egg

1 tablespoon water

CROSS PASTE

¼ cup bread flour

2 tablespoons milk

2 tablespoons shortening

1 tablespoon sugar

¼ teaspoon salt

SIMPLE SYRUP

1 cup granulated sugar

1 cup water

For dough:

1. Combine warm milk and yeast in a small bowl and set aside for 5 minutes.
2. Combine flour, sugar, salt, and cinnamon in the bowl of an electric mixer fitted with a dough hook attachment. Add egg, milk-yeast mixture, and raisins; mix on low speed for 2 minutes.
3. Add butter and mix on medium speed for 5 minutes, or until dough can be pulled without tearing.
4. Place dough on a floured surface and cover with a towel; set aside until doubled in size.

For egg wash:

Whisk together egg and water in a small bowl.

For cross paste:

While dough is rising, combine flour, milk, shortening, sugar, and salt; mix until smooth and set aside.

For simple syrup:

Combine sugar and water in small saucepan and bring to a boil. When sugar is dissolved remove from heat and cool.

(continued on page 20)

To serve:

1. With floured hands, divide dough into balls a little larger than a golf ball. Place balls on parchment paper, spacing 2 inches apart. Set aside to rise for 1 hour at room temperature.

2. Preheat oven to 350°F. Lightly brush buns with egg wash with a pastry brush. Place cross paste in a piping bag or a zip-top bag. Cut small hole in the corner of the bag and pipe an "X" on top of each bun.

3. Bake 12 minutes, or until golden brown. While buns are still warm, brush with simple syrup.

Coconut-Crusted Tofu in Miso Broth

The Hollywood Brown Derby ❄ Disney's Hollywood Studios ❄ Walt Disney World Resort

Earth Day started in 1970 in the U.S. to inspire appreciation for the Earth's natural ecosystem, and today it's a worldwide event on the first day of spring. Celebrate with this vegan dish that amazingly transforms tofu with coconut and curry.

Serves 4

MISO BROTH

4 cups water

½ cup tomato juice

1 (2-inch) piece fresh ginger, sliced

1 stalk lemongrass, white part only, sliced

1 jalapeño, seeds removed and roughly chopped

1 garlic clove, smashed

2 tablespoons rice vinegar

2 tablespoons soy sauce

1 teaspoon sesame oil

¼ cup white miso paste

3 tablespoons red curry paste

COCONUT-CRUSTED TOFU

4 ounces firm tofu

⅓ cup shredded coconut

1 ½ tablespoons cornstarch

1 ½ tablespoons all-purpose flour

Vegetable oil, for frying

4 heads baby bok choy, halved

1 cup sliced shiitake mushrooms

1 cup snow pea pods

8 ounces fresh Chinese egg noodles

Sliced green onions, for garnish

For miso broth:

1. Combine water, tomato juice, ginger, lemongrass, jalapeño, garlic, rice vinegar, soy sauce, and sesame oil in a large saucepan over medium heat.

2. When mixture is warm, whisk in miso paste and red curry paste. Cook 30 minutes, stirring occasionally. Strain broth through a fine-mesh sieve and return to pot.

For coconut-crusted tofu:

1. Place two layers of paper towels on a large, flat plate. Place tofu on paper towels and place another two layers of paper towels on top of tofu. Place another flat plate on top, and weigh plate down with a large can or heavy book. Press 15 minutes.

2. Cut pressed tofu in half through the middle to create 2 thinner blocks, then cut each of the pieces into quarters. Set aside.

3. Combine coconut, cornstarch, and flour in a shallow bowl. Dredge tofu pieces in coconut mixture, pressing to adhere.

4. Heat vegetable oil in a large sauté pan over medium until it shimmers. Add coconut-crusted tofu to oil in one layer and cook just until coconut is golden, about 2 to 3 minutes each side. Place on a plate lined with paper towels.

To serve:

1. Place bok choy, shiitakes, snow peas, and noodles in hot miso broth. Simmer until noodles are cooked through and vegetables are just tender.

2. Divide vegetables and noodles evenly among 4 serving bowls. Top with coconut-crusted tofu. Garnish with green onions.

MOTHER'S DAY

Sweet Potato Pancakes with Honey-Pecan Butter

THE WAVE . . . OF AMERICAN FLAVORS ❇ DISNEY'S CONTEMPORARY RESORT ❇ WALT DISNEY WORLD RESORT

2 ¼ cups all-purpose flour

3 teaspoons baking powder

¼ teaspoon ground cinnamon

¼ teaspoon ground nutmeg

¼ teaspoon salt

1 ½ cups milk

1 ¼ cups brown sugar

¾ cup cooked, mashed sweet potato (from about 1 small sweet potato)

3 large eggs

3 tablespoons vegetable oil

1 teaspoon vanilla extract

½ cup butter, at room temperature

¼ cup honey

¼ cup chopped toasted pecans

Make Mom an extra special breakfast in bed for Mother's Day with these pancakes and crunchy sweet butter.

SERVES 4 TO 6

1. Preheat oven to 225°F.
2. Sift flour into a large bowl. Add baking powder, cinnamon, nutmeg, and salt, and whisk until combined.
3. Combine milk, brown sugar, sweet potato, eggs, vegetable oil, and vanilla extract in a large bowl; whisk until well blended. Add milk mixture to flour mixture, and stir until just blended.
4. Heat a nonstick griddle or skillet over medium-low heat until a few drops of water sizzle on the surface. If using an electric skillet, preheat to 350°F.
5. Spoon about ¼ cup of batter per pancake onto skillet. Cook on first side until tops bubble and sides look dry; flip and cook until golden brown, about 2 minutes more.
6. Place cooked pancakes on a baking sheet and place into preheated oven to keep warm. Repeat process with remaining batter.
7. Stir together butter, honey, and pecans in a medium bowl.
8. Top pancakes with honey-pecan butter, and serve immediately.

Coffee

Goofy's Kitchen Cherry Tomato and Bocconcini Salad

GOOFY'S KITCHEN ❊ DISNEYLAND HOTEL ❊ DISNEYLAND RESORT

A quick and easy combo of tomatoes and mozzarella cheese is the perfect Memorial Day picnic salad. Bocconcini are egg-sized mozzarella balls, but you can use any sort of fresh mozzarella in this salad.

SERVES 6

- 1/3 cup thinly sliced red onion
- 2 tablespoons golden balsamic vinegar or sherry balsamic vinegar, divided
- 4 cups cherry tomatoes, halved
- 2 cups bocconcini, drained and halved
- 2 tablespoons thinly sliced basil
- 2 tablespoons olive oil
- 1 teaspoon coarse salt
- 1/4 teaspoon freshly ground black pepper

1. Combine onions and 1 tablespoon vinegar in a medium bowl; toss to combine. Set aside for 20 minutes. Drain onions from vinegar and set aside; discard vinegar.

2. Combine tomatoes and bocconcini in a large bowl. Add remaining 1 tablespoon vinegar, drained onions, basil, and olive oil. Season with salt and pepper and toss to combine.

FATHER'S DAY

Grilled Santa Maria Tri-Tip

ARIEL'S GROTTO ❊ DISNEY CALIFORNIA ADVENTURE PARK ❊ DISNEYLAND RESORT

TRI-TIP

1 tablespoon coarse salt

1 tablespoon freshly ground black pepper

1 tablespoon granulated garlic

1 ½ pounds tri-tip steak

WHITE CHEDDAR MASHED POTATOES

2 pounds Yukon gold potatoes

Coarse salt, to taste

1 cup heavy cream

4 cloves roasted garlic

4 tablespoons unsalted butter

2 cups shredded white cheddar cheese

Freshly ground black pepper, to taste

PICO DE GALLO

4 tomatoes, diced small

1 chipotle chili, finely chopped

2 tablespoons roughly chopped fresh cilantro

2 green onions, sliced

2 teaspoons coarse salt

2 limes, juiced

Grilling is a natural for Father's Day, and Santa Maria tri-tip, also known as sirloin tip, is a delicious change of pace. With origins in the town of Santa Maria, California, which was originally settled by Mexican cowboys, this dish is served with a kicky pico de gallo and creamy potatoes. If you don't want to smoke the beef, it's also delicious simply grilled.

SERVES 4

For tri-tip:

1. Combine salt, pepper, and garlic in a small bowl. Generously season the steak on both sides. Set aside. Prepare a smoke box by soaking 2 generous handfuls of hardwood chips in water for 30 minutes. Place soaked chips in a disposable aluminum pan.

2. Preheat an outdoor grill to high. Place the steak on the grill fat side down and sear 5 minutes. Flip steak and sear 2 to 3 minutes more.

3. If using a charcoal grill, carefully remove the grate and mound coals to one side of the grill. Place the prepared smoke box opposite the coals. Replace grate.

4. If using a gas grill, turn on one side of the grill. Remove the grate, and place the smoke box over the flame.

5. Place steak on the side of the grill that is not on, and smoke for 20 to 25 minutes, or until an instant-read thermometer reaches 125°F. Rest steak for at least 10 minutes.

6. Thinly slice steak against the grain just before serving.

(continued on page 28)

For white cheddar mashed potatoes:

1. Peel potatoes and cut into large pieces. Place in a large pot and fill with cold water. Bring to a boil; stir in a few generous pinches of salt. Reduce to a simmer and cook until potatoes are fork tender.

2. Meanwhile, combine cream, roasted garlic, and butter in a small saucepan over low heat.

3. Strain potatoes from water; return potatoes to pot and add warm cream mixture. Mash until almost smooth; add cheddar. Continue mashing until completely smooth. Season to taste with salt and pepper.

For pico de gallo:

Wash and dice tomatoes and place in a medium bowl. Add chipotle, cilantro, green onions, salt, and lime juice; stir gently to combine. Serve over grilled tri-tip.

What to drink: World-class Caymus Vineyards Cabernet Sauvignon from Napa Valley matches perfectly with the steak and pico de gallo, with complex layers of dark chocolate, blackberry, and leather.

Roasted Garlic-Orange Pork Ribs with Corn Slaw

CARNATION CAFÉ ❊ DISNEYLAND PARK ❊ DISNEYLAND RESORT

The Fourth of July calls for a cookout, and this irresistible rib-slaw combo feeds a hungry crowd. Fresh roasted summertime corn adds panache to an easy slaw.

SERVES 4

For roasted garlic-orange barbecue sauce:

1. Preheat oven to 400°F. Drizzle oil over garlic, and wrap with foil. Bake for 20 to 25 minutes, or until garlic cloves are soft. Allow to cool and squeeze cloves out of their skins into a medium bowl. Mash with a fork into a paste.
2. Add barbecue sauce, honey, orange zest, and sugar, and stir to combine. Refrigerate overnight.

For ribs:

1. Place ribs in baking dish. Combine Cajun seasoning and brown sugar; rub on ribs. Cover and refrigerate ribs overnight.
2. Preheat oven to 350°F. Uncover and add water to baking dish. Cover tightly with foil and bake for 35 minutes.
3. Generously brush ribs with barbecue sauce and place on preheated outdoor grill. Cook, covered, 15 minutes. Uncover, baste ribs with more sauce, and cook 15 minutes, uncovered, or until ribs are tender.

For roasted corn slaw:

1. Preheat oven to 450°F. Place corn on baking sheet and roast 15 to 20 minutes, or until golden brown.
2. Combine roasted corn, cabbage, carrots, red pepper, and chives; season with salt and pepper. Toss until combined, then stir in dressing.
3. Refrigerate 15 to 20 minutes before serving.

WHAT TO DRINK: Frog's Leap Zinfandel from Napa Valley balances the barbecue and garlic flavors with blueberry and raspberry and touches of cinnamon and white pepper.

ROASTED GARLIC-ORANGE BBQ SAUCE

1 head garlic, top ⅓ cut off

¼ teaspoon olive oil

2 ½ cups barbecue sauce

2 tablespoons honey

1 ½ tablespoons orange zest

1 teaspoon sugar

RIBS

4 pounds pork baby back ribs

4 tablespoons Cajun seasoning

2 tablespoons brown sugar

1 cup water

ROASTED CORN SLAW

2 cups corn kernels

1 pound shredded green cabbage

1 cup shredded carrots

1 cup chopped red pepper

½ cup chopped chives

½ teaspoon salt

¼ teaspoon crushed black pepper

½ cup purchased coleslaw dressing

HALLOWEEN

Jack Skellington Sugar Cookies

TONY'S TOWN SQUARE RESTAURANT ❄ MAGIC KINGDOM PARK ❄ WALT DISNEY WORLD RESORT

SUGAR COOKIES

2 ½ cups all-purpose flour

1 teaspoon baking powder

½ teaspoon salt

¾ cup butter, softened

1 cup sugar

2 eggs

½ teaspoon vanilla extract

ICING

2 egg whites

3 cups confectioners' sugar

½ teaspoon almond extract

Black food coloring paste

These spooky cookies are a sweet homemade treat for Halloween. For a shortcut, use slice-and-bake cookie dough.

MAKES 18 COOKIES

For sugar cookies:

1. Combine flour, baking powder, and salt in a medium bowl and whisk until combined. Set aside.

2. Combine butter and sugar in the bowl of an electric mixer and beat until smooth. Beat in eggs and vanilla. Add flour mixture in three parts. Once dough comes together, cover bowl with plastic wrap and refrigerate for at least 1 hour.

3. Preheat oven to 400°F.

4. On a floured surface, roll out dough to ¼-inch thickness. Using a round cookie cutter or an overturned cup, cut dough into circles about 3 ¼ inches in diameter. Place cookies 1 inch apart on an ungreased cookie sheet.

5. Bake 8 to 10 minutes, or until golden brown. Cool completely before icing.

For icing:

1. Place egg whites in bowl of an electric mixer; whisk until frothy. Add confectioners' sugar a little at a time, until thick but still spreadable.

2. Place one third of icing in a separate bowl. Add black food coloring paste to reserved icing and stir until color is uniform.

3. Decorate cooled cookies by covering with white icing and letting it dry (placing cookies in the refrigerator will speed up this process).

4. Place black icing in a pastry bag or a plastic resealable bag and cut off a tiny bit of the corner to create a very small hole. Use black icing to draw eyes, nostrils, and stitched mouth on each cookie.

Pumpkin-Ginger Soup with Milk Foam

❊ *Disney Cruise Line Services*

Think beyond traditional pumpkin pie and start Thanksgiving dinner with a sip of this creamy, rich soup. If you're in a hurry, you can substitute two cups of canned pumpkin for the fresh pumpkin. The fancy foam garnish and a flourish of nutmeg make it special.

Serves 10

- 2 ½ cups vegetable stock
- 12 tablespoons butter
- 2 onions, finely sliced
- 1 stalk celery, roughly chopped
- 2 tablespoons freshly grated ginger
- ½ cup all-purpose flour
- 1 (4-pound) pumpkin, peeled, seeded, and cubed
- 1 ¼ cups heavy cream
- ¾ cup apple juice
- Coarse salt and ground white pepper, to taste
- ¼ cup whole milk
- ¼ cup heavy cream
- Freshly grated nutmeg, for garnish

1. Heat vegetable stock in a small saucepan.
2. Melt butter in a stockpot over medium heat; add onions and sauté for about 2 minutes. Add celery and ginger and sauté 2 minutes longer. Sprinkle flour over mixture and cook, stirring constantly, for 3 minutes.
3. Pour in hot vegetable stock and bring to a boil, whisking any lumps that form. Reduce heat to medium, add cubed pumpkin, and simmer 30 minutes, stirring frequently to keep soup from scorching.
4. Add heavy cream and apple juice and simmer for 20 minutes longer, stirring often.
5. Once the pumpkin is very tender, puree soup with an immersion blender or with a regular blender, working in 2 batches. (If soup is too thick, use vegetable stock to thin.) Season to taste with salt and white pepper. Strain soup through a fine-mesh sieve.
6. To make foam garnish, combine milk and cream in a small saucepan over medium heat until hot but not boiling. Whip with an immersion blender until foamy, similar to a cappuccino. Ladle soup into a bowl; spoon a small amount of foam in the center of the soup. Garnish with freshly grated nutmeg and serve immediately.

THANKSGIVING

Sweet Potato Gnocchi with Honey-Caper Brown Butter

ARTIST POINT ❄ DISNEY'S WILDERNESS LODGE ❄ WALT DISNEY WORLD RESORT

GNOCCHI

1 pound sweet potatoes

2 to 3 cups all-purpose flour

1 egg yolk

½ teaspoon coarse salt

HONEY-CAPER BROWN BUTTER

1 stick butter, sliced into tablespoon pieces

2 tablespoons honey

1 tablespoon capers

1 teaspoon truffle oil

Coarse salt, freshly ground black pepper, to taste

Gnocchi (*nyoh-kee)* are Italian-style dumplings—fluffy "little pillows." This slightly sweet gnocchi is made with sweet potatoes—perfect for the winter holidays.

SERVES 4

For gnocchi:

1. Preheat oven to 450°F. Pierce potatoes all over with a sharp knife and bake until tender, about 45 minutes to 1 hour. Set aside to cool to room temperature.

2. Peel potatoes, cut into pieces, and push through a potato ricer into a large bowl.

3. Make a well in the center of mashed sweet potatoes, and add 2 cups flour, egg yolk, and salt. Mix, adding more flour if needed, until a soft dough forms. Dough should be soft but not sticky.

4. Divide dough into 6 equal balls. On a floured surface, roll each ball into a 1-inch wide rope. Cut each rope into 1-inch pieces. Transfer the formed gnocchi to a large baking sheet. Continue with remaining gnocchi.

5. Bring a large pot of salted water to a rolling boil. Cook gnocchi, working in 3 batches, until tender but still firm, stirring occasionally, about 5 minutes. Drain onto a baking sheet, using a slotted spoon. Tent with foil to keep warm and continue with remaining gnocchi.

For honey-caper brown butter:

1. While gnocchi are cooking, melt butter in heavy-bottomed skillet over medium-high heat, whisking constantly. Watch carefully as butter cooks and begins to turn light brown in color. As soon as butter begins to turn brown and smell nutty, remove skillet from heat.

2. Stir in honey and capers (mixture may bubble). Finish with truffle oil. Check for seasoning and add salt and pepper to taste.

3. To serve, drizzle over cooked gnocchi.

WHAT TO DRINK: The rich raspberry and truffle flavors in King Estate Pinot Noir from Oregon match the mushrooms and sweet potatoes.

Gingerbread Cookies

DISNEY'S GRAND FLORIDIAN RESORT & SPA ❇ WALT DISNEY WORLD RESORT

Old-fashioned and delicious, these cookies help create the life-size gingerbread house at *Disney's Grand Floridian* Resort & Spa. Guests buy them to carry home, and now you can bake your own for sharing. You'll find star anise in the ethnic aisle of your local grocery store. To get the best flavor, you need to grind the whole star anise pod.

MAKES 3 DOZEN COOKIES

2 sticks (1 cup) butter, softened

2 ½ cups confectioners' sugar, sifted

2 eggs

3 ⅔ cups all-purpose flour

2 ½ teaspoons ground cinnamon

2 ¼ teaspoons ground coriander

2 teaspoons ground star anise

1 ¼ teaspoons baking powder

1 teaspoon ground fennel

1 teaspoon ground ginger

1 teaspoon ground cloves

½ teaspoon salt

¼ teaspoon ground mace

¼ cup milk

1 cup colored decorating sugar

1. Combine butter and sugar in bowl of electric mixer and beat until smooth. Beat in eggs.
2. Sift together flour, cinnamon, coriander, anise, baking powder, fennel, ginger, cloves, salt, and mace into a separate large bowl.
3. With mixer on low, slowly add dry ingredients to butter mixture until dough holds together.
4. Remove dough from bowl and wrap in plastic wrap; refrigerate until firm, 2 to 4 hours.
5. Preheat oven to 350°F and grease 2 cookie sheets.
6. Remove dough from refrigerator and set aside at room temperature for about 10 minutes, until pliable. Divide dough in half; return one half to refrigerator. Place the other half on a floured work surface. Roll dough to ⅛-inch thickness, flouring the work surface and rolling pin as needed.
7. Cut out cookies with cookie cutters (dip cutters in flour for neat edges). Transfer to baking sheets, 1 inch apart.
8. Lightly brush cookies with milk and sprinkle with colored sugar.
9. Bake until firm and edges begin to darken, 10 to 14 minutes. Allow cookies to slightly cool on cookie sheet, then transfer to wire racks to completely cool. Repeat with remaining dough.

HANUKKAH

Smoked-Salmon-and-Herb Muffins

DISNEY'S CORONADO SPRINGS RESORT CATERING ❄ WALT DISNEY WORLD RESORT

1 1/4 cups all-purpose flour

1 tablespoon baking powder

1/4 teaspoon salt

1/4 teaspoon ground pepper

1 cup mayonnaise

1 egg, beaten

1/2 cup, plus 1 tablespoon melted butter

1 cup milk

2 tablespoons chopped fresh dill

2 tablespoons chopped fresh chives

1/2 cup cream cheese

2 tablespoons capers

12 thin slices smoked salmon

Fresh dill sprigs

Muffins with fresh dill and chives are baked and then stuffed with a mixture of cream cheese, smoked salmon, capers, and dill, an easy dish for a Hanukkah brunch.

MAKES 24 MINIMUFFINS

1. Preheat oven to 400°F. Spray minimuffin tins with nonstick spray.
2. Sift together flour, baking powder, salt, and pepper into a large bowl.
3. In a separate bowl, whisk together mayonnaise, egg, melted butter, and milk. Stir in dill and chives.
4. Pour milk mixture into flour mixture and stir until just combined.
5. Fill muffin tins three-quarters full with batter. Bake 25 to 35 minutes, until golden. Transfer to wire rack to cool.
6. Combine cream cheese and capers. Cut muffins in half widthwise. Spread each half with cream cheese mixture, top with a folded slice of smoked salmon, and top that with dill sprig, then sandwich together. Serve at room temperature.

Curry Chicken with Jollaf Rice

Tusker House Restaurant ❊ Disney's Animal Kingdom Park ❊ Walt Disney World Resort

For a Kwanzaa celebration, create an African-inspired dish. The December holiday honors African American heritage and culture.

Serves 4

For Cape Malay chicken:

1. Season chicken with salt and pepper. Heat olive oil in large, heavy skillet over medium-high heat and sear chicken until golden brown on all sides, about 5 minutes; set chicken aside.

2. Heat vegetable oil in a large stockpot over medium-high heat; add onions and sauté until translucent, about 3 minutes. Add garlic, jalapeños, and ginger; sauté for 30 seconds, then turn heat to low. Cook for 15 minutes, stirring occasionally, making sure nothing browns or burns.

3. Add curry powder, paprika, and curry paste, and cook 5 minutes over low heat, stirring gently. Sprinkle in a few drops of water if needed to keep mixture from burning.

4. Add flour and stir mixture 5 minutes.

5. Add ½ cup tomato juice, stir to combine, and remove from heat.

6. Place remaining ½ cup tomato juice in a blender; add the contents of stockpot and canned tomatoes. Blend until smooth.

7. Return pureed mixture to stockpot over low heat and cook 30 minutes, stirring occasionally.

8. Add seared chicken and cook 10 to 15 minutes, seasoning with salt and pepper.

(continued on page 40)

CAPE MALAY CHICKEN

2 pounds boneless chicken thighs, diced

1 tablespoon coarse salt, plus additional to taste

1 teaspoon freshly ground black pepper, plus additional to taste

2 tablespoons olive oil

6 tablespoons vegetable oil

2 medium onions, coarsely chopped (about 2 cups)

8 garlic cloves, peeled and sliced

2 jalapeños, seeds removed and chopped

1 (3-inch) piece fresh ginger, peeled and thinly sliced

2 teaspoons madras curry powder

1 tablespoon paprika

1 teaspoon mild red curry paste

¼ cup all-purpose flour

1 cup tomato juice, divided

14.5-ounce can chopped tomatoes

JOLLAF RICE

2 cups chicken stock

¼ cup tomato juice

1 small onion, diced

1 sprig rosemary, chopped

1 sprig thyme, chopped

1 ½ teaspoons red curry paste

1 ½ teaspoons paprika

1 ½ teaspoons granulated garlic

1 ½ teaspoons turmeric

2 tomatoes, diced

1 cup long-grain white rice

¼ cup olive oil

For Jollaf rice:

1. Combine chicken stock, tomato juice, onion, rosemary, thyme, red curry paste, paprika, granulated garlic, and turmeric in a large saucepan over high heat; bring to a boil. Stir in tomatoes and rice.
2. Cover and turn heat to low. Cook 20 minutes, or until rice is cooked and all liquid is absorbed.
3. Drizzle in oil, fluffing with a fork.
4. Serve chicken over rice.

What to drink: Rudera Chenin Blanc from South Africa balances the spice in the curry chicken.

Roast Duck with Sweet Onion Popovers

CLUB 33 ❇ DISNEYLAND PARK ❇ DISNEYLAND RESORT

Crispy roast duck is a favorite Christmas feast. Instead of stuffing, serve with sweet, fluffy onion popovers.

SERVES 4

DUCK

1 (5- to 6-pound) duck

1 large onion, peeled and roughly chopped

1 celery stalk, roughly chopped

1 large carrot, roughly chopped

1 bay leaf

6 sprigs fresh thyme

1 teaspoon coarse salt

½ teaspoon freshly ground black pepper

2 tablespoons unsalted butter, softened

NATURAL PAN JUS

1 large onion, peeled and roughly chopped

2 carrots, roughly chopped

2 celery stalks, roughly chopped

1 garlic head, cut in half lengthwise

¼ cup dry red wine, such as merlot or cabernet sauvignon

1 bay leaf

8 sprigs fresh thyme

1 cup chicken stock

For duck:

1. Preheat oven to 400°F.
2. Rinse duck under cold running water. Remove gizzards from the body cavity. Remove and discard excess fat and place duck breast-side up in a roasting pan.
3. Toss together onion, celery, carrot, bay leaf, and thyme; stuff mixture into cavity of duck. Prick skin all over with a sharp fork; season with salt and pepper. Tie legs together, then rub with butter.
4. Roast duck, uncovered, for 1 hour. Transfer duck to a large plate and pour juices from roasting pan into a medium bowl. Reserve juices.
5. Return duck to pan, prick skin again with a sharp fork, and continue cooking for 1 hour. Pour off any juice from pan into bowl. Return duck to pan and cook 45 minutes longer, or until meat is very tender and skin is crisp.
6. Remove from oven and let sit in roasting pan 10 minutes before carving.

For pan jus:

1. While duck is roasting, skim and discard fat from pan juices. Combine onion, carrots, celery, garlic, and skimmed pan juices in a medium saucepan over medium heat.
2. Cook until vegetables are tender, about 10 minutes, stirring occasionally.
3. Add wine and continue to cook until sauce is reduced by three fourths. Add bay leaf and thyme.

(continued on page 42)

SWEET ONION POPOVERS

1 (1-pound) loaf brioche or egg bread

1 tablespoon butter

½ cup small diced sweet onions

4 eggs

2 teaspoons sugar

2 teaspoons chopped fresh thyme

4 cups heavy cream

4. Add chicken stock and cook for about 15 minutes, until sauce is reduced to the consistency of light syrup.

5. Strain sauce through a fine-mesh sieve and serve alongside duck.

For popovers:

1. Cut bread into 1-inch cubes and leave at room temperature, uncovered, for 1 hour.

2. Preheat oven to 350°F. Lightly coat a muffin pan with nonstick cooking spray.

3. Melt butter in a sauté pan over medium heat; add onions and cook until translucent, 3 to 4 minutes. Set aside to cool completely.

4. Whisk together eggs, sugar, thyme, and cream. Stir in onions.

5. Add bread cubes and toss to combine. Set aside for 15 minutes, tossing occasionally.

6. Place bread mixture into each muffin cup, filling just to the top. Bake 20 to 25 minutes, or until the centers are completely cooked. (Use a toothpick to pierce the center, and if it come out clean, popovers are ready.)

7. Cool completely in muffin pan.

What to drink: Flowers Vineyard & Winery's Pinot Noir, from California's Sonoma coast, complements the roast duck with elegant flavors of cherry, spice, and olives.

Vegetable Tamales

RANCHO DEL ZOCALO RESTAURANTE ❊ DISNEYLAND PARK ❊ DISNEYLAND RESORT

For many, tamales are a delicious Christmas Eve repast. The process of making food with family and friends is part of the endearing tradition. *Masa harina*, Spanish for "corn flour," is made from sun- or fire-dried corn kernels, and may be found in the ethnic aisle of grocery stores or in specialty markets.

MAKES 18 TAMALES

VEGETABLE FILLING

4 large fresh pasilla or poblano peppers

2 medium russet potatoes

4 medium carrots

½ (1-pound) bag frozen sweet peas

2 pounds *queso fresco* (fresh cheese)

TAMALE DOUGH

3 ½ cups *masa harina*

1 tablespoon coarse salt

1 ½ teaspoons baking powder

½ cup lard or vegetable shortening, at room temperature

2 to 4 cups chicken broth

TAMALE WRAPPERS

24 dried corn husks, soaked in a sink filled with warm water for 30 minutes to soften

Favorite chili sauce or salsa, for serving

For vegetable filling:

1. Place peppers on a baking sheet lined with foil. Place under a preheated broiler, about 2 inches below the heat. Broil until skin blisters and is charred, turning evenly to char.

2. Place peppers in a bowl and cover tightly with plastic wrap. Steam in bowl for about 5 minutes, then gently peel away skin. Cut off tops of peppers and discard stems and seeds. Cut peppers into strips about 3 inches long and a ½-inch wide.

3. Peel potatoes and place in bowl of cold water. Cut each potato into sections 3 inches long, a ½-inch wide, and a ½-inch thick (like steak fries). Return potato sections to water until ready to use.

4. Peel carrots and cut into sections 3 inches long, a ½-inch wide, and a ½-inch thick.

5. Place frozen peas in a sieve and run under hot water until bright green.

6. Crumble cheese in a small bowl.

(continued on page 44)

For tamale dough:

1. Place *masa harina*, salt, baking powder, and shortening in bowl of an electric mixer fitted with paddle attachment. Blend until shortening is evenly distributed.

2. Mix in chicken broth, a cup at a time, until the consistency is that of mashed potatoes.

For tamales:

1. Rinse, drain, and dry corn husks. Lay 1 corn husk, concave-side up, on a work surface. Place about 2 tablespoons tamale dough in a thin, even layer across the wide end of the husk. Dough should be about a ½ inch from the sides, 1 inch from the top, and about 3 inches from the bottom.

2. Place 2 strips pepper, 1 piece potato, 1 piece carrot, 1 teaspoon peas, and 1 teaspoon cheese in center of dough. Bring sides up to meet, pinching dough to seal, and then roll tamale into a cylinder. Fold bottom of husk up and under. Set tamale seam-side down on a baking sheet or large platter. Repeat with remaining ingredients.

3. Add a few inches water to a large stockpot and place a steamer basket inside. Place tamales in steamer, stacking no more than 2. Place pot over high heat and bring water to a boil, then lower heat to medium-low. Steam tamales for about 90 minutes, or until the tamales start to pull away from husks and filling is soft, firm, and not mushy. (Check to make sure water doesn't boil away.)

4. To serve, unfold the husk and top with favorite chili sauce or salsa.

What to drink: With tropical fruit and floral aromas, Conundrum, a blend of California white grapes, accentuates the spices in the tamales.

CHRISTMAS

Yule Log

CAPE MAY CAFÉ AND YACHTSMAN STEAKHOUSE ❊ *DISNEY'S YACHT & BEACH CLUB* RESORTS ❊ *WALT DISNEY WORLD* RESORT

A classic Christmas dessert, the Yule Log, or Bûche de Noël, carries on the tradition of celebrating Christmas and the winter solstice by burning a wooden log in the hearth. In the late 1800s, a French pastry chef came up with the idea of replacing the real Yule log with a log-shaped cake.

SERVES 10

CHOCOLATE CHIFFON CAKE

½ cup all-purpose flour

2 tablespoons cocoa powder

⅓ cup, plus 3 teaspoons, sugar, divided

1 teaspoon baking powder

¼ teaspoon salt

1 egg

2 teaspoons vegetable oil

2 teaspoons milk

½ teaspoon vanilla extract

2 egg whites

Pinch cream of tartar

CHOCOLATE MOUSSE CREMÉUX

2 eggs, separated

2 tablespoons, plus 2 teaspoons, sugar, divided

6 ounces dark chocolate, finely chopped

3 tablespoons butter

½ cup heavy cream

For chiffon cake:

1. Preheat oven to 350°F. Coat a 13x9x2-inch baking pan with nonstick spray. Measure and cut a piece of parchment paper to line bottom of pan and spray with nonstick spray.

2. Sift together flour, cocoa powder, ⅓ cup sugar, baking powder, and salt, and place in bowl of an electric mixer fitted with paddle attachment. With mixer running at slow speed, add egg, oil, milk, and vanilla extract one at a time, scraping bowl after each addition until mixture is smooth. Transfer batter to a large bowl.

3. After thoroughly cleaning mixer bowl, combine egg whites, remaining 3 teaspoons sugar, and cream of tartar. Whip on high speed until soft peaks form. Fold one third of egg white mixture into cake batter, then fold remaining egg white mixture into batter.

4. Spread batter evenly into prepared pan. Batter will be only ¼-inch deep. Bake 6 to 10 minutes, just until set. *Do not overbake.*

5. Remove cake from oven, let cool for 10 minutes. While cake is still warm, slide it out of pan, with parchment still attached, onto a clean kitchen towel. Trim crispy edges off the long sides of the cake. Beginning at one narrow end, use the towel to roll cake—along with parchment paper—into a cylinder.

(continued on page 47)

For mousse:

1. Combine egg yolks and 2 tablespoons sugar in a large bowl; whisk until light in color and thickened, about 3 minutes.

2. Fill a medium saucepan about halfway with water. Bring water to a simmer. Combine chocolate and butter in a heatproof bowl and place bowl over simmering water, making sure bowl does not touch water.

3. Stir chocolate mixture constantly until completely melted. Remove from heat and set aside to cool slightly.

4. When chocolate mixture is room temperature, stir into egg yolk mixture.

5. Place egg whites in the bowl of an electric mixer fitted with whisk attachment. Beat until frothy, then add remaining 2 teaspoons sugar, beating until medium peaks form.

6. Whip heavy cream on high speed until soft peaks form.

7. Gently fold egg white mixture into chocolate mixture, then gently fold in whipped cream. (Some streaks of cream may remain; do not overmix.) Refrigerate until cold.

For ganache:

Place chocolate in a large heatproof bowl. Heat heavy cream in a medium saucepan over medium heat until hot but not boiling. Whisk in cream until combined. Set aside until slightly cool but still spreadable.

To serve:

1. Carefully unroll cake from towel; remove towel. Spread mousse over cake surface. Using parchment paper to lift up a narrow edge of the cake, roll it back up, over the mousse, peeling off parchment paper as you go.

2. Once cake is rolled, wrap parchment paper around it to keep it round and place cake seam-side down on a platter. Refrigerate about 1 hour, until firm.

3. Remove parchment paper from cake and ice with ganache. Sprinkle with crushed peppermint candy. Refrigerate until ganache is set, about 30 minutes, before serving.

CHOCOLATE GANACHE

8 ounces dark chocolate

3/4 cup heavy cream

Crushed peppermint candy, for garnish

Acknowledgments

As always, the biggest thanks goes to Karen McClintock, who brings tremendous energy to the cookbook projects. Also to Katie Farmand and Jessie Ward, recipe testers extraordinaire, and to Katie for photo styling and Jessie for editing skills. To Gary Bogdon for his beautiful photography that brings the book to life, and to designer Jon Glick, who synchronizes the beauty. To the Disney Chefs for their creativity in the kitchen, and to Disney sommelier Jason Cha-Kim for his expert beverage pairings. To Betsy Singer and Aaron Babcock in Disney Theme Park Merchandise for their support. And extra special thanks to editorial director Wendy Lefkon.

For information address Disney Editions, 114 Fifth Avenue, New York, NY 10011-5690.
Editorial Director: Wendy Lefkon
Associate Editor: Jessica Ward
Designed by: Jon Glick, mouse+tiger
ISBN 978-1-4231-4534-9
F850-6835-5-12121
First Edition
Reinforced binding
10 9 8 7 6 5 4 3 2 1
Printed in Singapore